Leadership: Discover & Maximize Your Leadership Style!

SADANAND PUJARI

Published by SADANAND PUJARI, 2024.

Table of Contents

Copyright 1

About 2

Introduction 4

Leaders Design Their Destiny 6

Leaders Fight For An Objective 7

Leaders Live With Crystal Clarity 9

Leadership Is Directly Linked To Your Capacity For Change 11

Leaders Are Always Striving For The Common Good Of Everyone Around Them! 13

Leadership Exacts A Price 15

Every Leader Begins With This Primordial Question - What Is My 17

Leaders Pay Heed To Their Inner Voice 19

There Is Difference Between Self-Awareness And Self-Delusion 20

Leadership Is A Self-Taught Path That Is Anchored In Reflection 22

Leaders Are Generators Of Tremendous Value - Followers Merely 24

Intellectual Horsepower Is Key To The Drive Of A Leader ..26

On A Spectrum Between Doers And Dreamers, Where Do You Fall?..28

Leaders Never Hit Rock Bottom, They Use It As A Springboard To Bounce Back..30

Leaders Thrive Or Melt Under Pressure 32

Singular Benefits Of Leadership..34

Leadership Is Both Substance And Style 35

Leadership Is Built On These Two Principles Of Physics 37

It Is Never About Being A Superhero, In Reality.....................38

It's About Not Being Blindsided 39

Leadership Is About Solving The Gaps 40

It Affects Your Whole Person, This Leadership Quest 42

You Could Be The Biggest Barrier To Your Growth 43

There Is No I In Leader...44

Have You Ever Thought About When It Is A Good Time To Grow As A Leader? 45

Leadership Is Never About One Definitive Answer 46

Leadership Is Launching Into The Unknown............................47

U Don't Jump The Seas In One Big Leap 48

Leadership Is Built On The Bedrock Of Confidence 49

Is There Anything New Under The Sun? 50

Leadership Is The Sum Total Of The Problems Solved 52

Explore These Ideas For The Fundamentals Of Leadership .. 53

Leadership Is Growth - Are You Prepared For The Growth Pangs 54

Leaders Are A Series Of Decisions - Good And Bad 55

Leadership Is A Choice 56

Four Benefits From This Book 57

Why Is This Book Different 58

You Can Run On Yesterday's Diet 60

Leadership Myths - No One Is Born A Leader 61

Leaders Are Not Made Based On Degree Or Pedigree 62

Leadership Myths - They Don't Always Have To Be Charismatic 64

A Great Leader Does Not Have To Manipulate People Around 65

Leaders Are Not Managers 67

A Must Possess Quality For The Future, To Shine In The Business World 68

Another Must-Have Trait For The Future Leader 70

A Leader Knows The Difference Between A Critic And A Coach 72

An Inspiring Leader Is Also Unreasonable 73

A Good Leader Is Bold Not A Bully 74

This Leader Runs From Cheating - Self 75

A Good Leader Knows The Difference Between A Learned Man And Learner 77

A Fine Leader Knows The Opposite Of A Desire 78

The Pandemic Leveled The Playing Field 79

In The Beginning, There Was A Leader Who Said" Let There Be Light" 81

He/She Gets The Difference Between The Fundamental Competing 83

A Modern Leader Knows That He Needs To Ride High Or Lie Low 85

The New Age Leader Is A Digital Maestro 87

Leaders Are Measured For Performance 89

The New Age Leader Starts With Seeing The Invisible 91

The New Age Leader Has A Vision With A Deep Core And Broad 94

This Leader Lives By The Rule Book Definition 97

The Leader's Currency Is Influence - Moving People Through Example 99

A Leader Keeps Providing The Resources To Make Everyone Successful 102

There Is Always A Way Because This Leader Is Dynamic 104

It's Never About Time Management, Always About Priorities 106

This Guide Has An Unflappable Temperament In The Face Of Difficulties 109

It Is Always The Right Time To Do The Right Thing! 112

For A Truly Committed Leader The Spoils Come After A Labor Of Love! 114

This New Era Calls For New Paradigms - This One Is For You 116

Another Paradigm Shift For This Leader 118

A Critical Aspect Of These Leaders Is They Don't Fit The Mold 120

They Know The Why Aspect Of Their Compulsive Obsession To Win 122

A Leader Is A Communicator - With A Megaphone 125

Build, Build And Build Is The Mantra For Value Creation . 127

Multi-Pronged Strategy Is His Middle Name. Always Planning To Make 129

A Leader Has A Heart - And Often Is Not Afraid To Wear It On His Sleeve 132

The Fixer- Leader Is Always Asking The Question - How Can We Fix It And Up 134

A Leader Is Always Brokering, Partnering And Making Alliances 136

This New Age Leader Is A Pathfinder And Pathmaker 138

The Difference Between A Leader And Coach Is Exponential 140

Copyright

Copyright © 2024 by **SADANAND PUJARI**

All rights reserved. No part of this book may be reproduced, scanned, or distributed in any printed or electronic form without permission. Please do not participate in or encourage piracy of copyrighted materials in violation of the author's rights. Purchase only authorized editions.

Leadership: Discover & Maximize Your Leadership Style!

Navigate; Amplify Your Leadership Abilities, Become An Even Better Leader!

First Edition: Jun 2024

Book Design by **SADANAND PUJARI**

About

The world has changed overnight and every dimension of our life got upended in an unprecedented manner. How we work, how we buy, how we live and how we study have gone through a metamorphosis. Live now revolves around a screen - yet, the world slowly grinds on...

However, everything falls and rises on Leadership. Everything grows and shrinks on the efforts of a leader. Business growth, Corporate leadership or personal mastery is a result of concerted choices by a Leader. This Book sets the foundations and building blocks for someone who can rise from any situation into a growth-oriented leader. Right from young executives to seasoned professionals, everyone can potentially elevate their game for amplified impact. This Book is a result of practical insights, implementable actions and ideas that stick because of the practitioner's perspective.

Tighten your seatbelts and enjoy this exhilarating ride, because it will change your thinking, offer compelling alternatives for you to grapple with and reflect. The bottom-line, they say, is the bottom-line. The question you should ask is Will this make me a better thinker, action taker and change my bottom-line? If your leadership does not transform your skills into material success at either your business or at work, then all we had was an intellectual discussion.

So here's our promise. Invest yourself in this Book and watch your worldview be challenged. We are harnessing decades of experience into this Book and we assure you that these chapters will lead you on the path to success. See you at the top!

Introduction

Imagine living the life of your dreams. Leadership makes it possible. Imagine setting high standards for yourself as far as your success goes, and are concerned about going out and achieving them. This leadership book will set you up on that journey to get what you dream and set goals for imagined, working with people and rallying them around for a common cause. This leadership book will allow you to go out there, get the design and the destiny of your life, and in the process impact others as well through your leadership skills. Leadership is all about leading first for yourself and others due to everyone's mutual success. And this leadership book is all about that.

How do you identify your dreams, your desires, and then set milestones with discipline, with the diligence that is needed to go out and achieve them? This book, has nothing but the promise to make your potential come alive in the process, transforming yourself and transforming scores of lives around you, because that's what great leaders do, a big goal, get a life of their dreams. But in the process, they also inspire and impact everyone around them. If this encourages you, stay with us and see you on the summit of success.

Here's a quick win for you. Find a mentor. Find a group of people, call your advisers and make them a part of your inner circle. Leadership journey is a journey that is encouraged, built up on the shoulders of others. I would have never been able to achieve a fraction of what I've achieved in my two and a half decades of leadership journey.

If it were not for the fact of the indelible influence of mentors and a group of advisors from time to time, I might be the virtual mentor for you, sharing all these insights virtually in this class. But you need a bunch of people that you can trust, people that may or may not be at work, but somebody who could come along and be your mentor, be somebody with whom you can lean on four times of help when you are bewildered, mystified in a maze of options, somebody who can think along with you, ask the right questions and help you find clarity, because leadership is a journey that is inexact in that time.

You need somebody who can say, turn right, turn left. This is where you might want to go and give you those words of advice. So find a mentor, find a group of advisors who will help you on this leadership journey.

Leaders Design Their Destiny

Would you like to discover, develop and deploy your strengths for success? Do you want to just live out and find your core calling in your life and fulfill the destiny that you acknowledge to be in this competitive world?

If you are someone who is looking to develop your voice and live out your gifts and talents, then this leadership book is for you. At the end of this book, you will be so sure of what your colleague is, so sure of some of your gifts and strengths and that you are enthusiastically going out to pursue the life of your dreams.

If you are ready to embark on this exciting adventure of discovering your Mount Everest and going along with us to the top of the summit, this book is meant for you.

Leaders Fight For An Objective

The best definition of leadership I ever did, not in a business school that I did an MBA or from a leadership guru, but from an acting class at the end of class in the fundamentals of teaching, they always teach that every actor is fighting for an objective. And if you take that out of the world of theater and put it in the context of leadership, a leader is someone who is fighting for an objective. Think about every leadership city, whether it's in the sports field, whether it's in the political world, whether it's in the business world, whether it is entrepreneurship and or health care. Everyone is actually fighting for an objective. And great leaders understand that their very existence is owed to one big objective.

If there's anything that you can take away from this chapter, it is what is the objective that I am fighting for? What is the objective that my team is fighting for? What is the objective that my organization is fighting for? The mission, the vision, some of these fancy terms that we keep using in the business world. But simplify it. You will come down to an objective worth fighting for. And so I want to set this up as a leadership journey for you and say, what is the dream that you are fighting for? What is the desire, the flaming desire that drives you and for which you are willing to invest your energy, your time, your resources, your attention, your focus to accomplish that. And my life's journey has been built on fighting for that objective of using my transformed communication skills to transform the world. And ever since I was a young executive growing up in India, I was committed to that objective, that mission, that vision of impacting the world through my communication skills. What is the objective you are fighting for?

Leaders Live With Crystal Clarity

If this one promises a quick win, a takeaway for you that we will offer, right, that this book is clarity. Within a short time, you'll be able to walk away with this absolute clarity. What do you need to do with your precious life? You know, often one is confused, conflicted with the bewildering amount of choices that are around us, with the amount of time pressures that wait for our attention. And you're always doing things in the fog of war. You're not clear what needs to be done. And unfortunately, the more and more the screams wait for our attention and the media is inundating messages at us, one is always short on clarity. Ralph Waldo Emerson is said to have constantly asked his friends this question.

Since we met, what has become more clear to you? It could be any topic, but he would just ask this on the most reflective, thoughtful question since we last met. What has become more clear to you? And I want to borrow that to ask you this question. And as you are grappling with these chapters and the insights that come across in this leadership book, clarity is one essential barometer for success. If you don't have clarity, then you are running around with confusion. And there's a lot of pain that is caused in the process of communicating with others. Because if you're not clear in your head, how are you going to communicate with others around you, whether it's your boss, whether it's your colleagues, whether it's people that work with you, vendors, partners, absolute clarity in your mind about what you need to do and where you need to go.

Essentially, every year I set some goals for myself and say that this year's success to me looks like this. And I set out a bunch of goals. And I hope as you read this chapter, you will start putting down a marker and saying, I need to get absolute clarity in my own life about the following areas and then start writing down these goals, these milestones that you need to achieve with the clarity that you are seeking for your life. Let me conclude by asking you this question. What is becoming clear about you in your own life, whether it is your professional life or your personal life? Are there too many relationships that are draining your energy and are sapping you and they're pulling you down? Or are there some things at work that are bothering you that you need to sort of give it your attention and bring clarity to take a moment to reflect on the need for clarity in your life?

Leadership Is Directly Linked To Your Capacity For Change

What is your capacity for change? You know, if you are aspiring to be a leader, your growth capability or your ability to change and become a better version of yourself is directly a function of your capacity to change. Now, the word change is often a scary world because it means that you're moving from a set of behaviors to a new set of behaviors. But great leaders, Renaissance leaders, new age leaders are those who are committed to improving themselves on a daily basis. And it is in that commitment lies our capacity for change. Are you committed to change, changing your mindset, changing your heart, changing your behaviors, perceiving how you behave in a sort of given conditions and trying to modify that for a higher purpose? Your capacity to change determines your ability to change and change quickly.

You know, we often change either because of the rewards and the joys of the prizes that go with the change behavior or the pain that comes from not changing the costs that you're paying because you did not change. If you want a young and upcoming leader, then if you want to change, if you want to take advantage of the promotion opportunities, the opportunities to lead large teams, large projects. So there is that reward in itself. They extend the extrinsic reward of changing. But it is also possible that you were forced to change because you are already in the leadership position and you are not able to handle the challenges that go along with it because you are not set up for change.

So a leader always changes in the sense a leader constantly is looking to see what are the things that he can change within his own sphere of influence so that others can also change their spheres of influence. And together, a ripple effect happens. So I want to ask you this. In the past, how fast were you and adapt to change? Did it happen because it happened? You had to have to change because you no longer had an option or you were a willing and enthusiastic student of learning who was willing to change.

There are two kinds of leaders in this world who are constantly, proactively learning to modify their behaviors. And then there are those who are coming to a point of need and then they are forced to change. Which one of these two are you? Are you this fast, enthusiastic, keen learner? I hope so. If not, you want to be one fast learning and enthusiastic, keen student of leadership.

Leaders Are Always Striving For The Common Good Of Everyone Around Them!

Every leader. Needs to find a definition of what is good for not just himself or herself, but for everyone around them. It is in that quest that common good leadership expresses itself. You know, often we see these highly ambitious, talented, gifted individuals just on one single minded pursuit, which is of self-interest. Most leaders come in by asking the question, what's in it for me? In the sense that as leaders, when they succeed or not, as leaders, when the stakes are high, will they be able to deliver the desired results or not? But that's only one part of the leadership.

Great leaders ask the question, is it in the interest of the common good common ground? We talk a lot about what is the collective good, what is the organizational work and so on and so forth. But leaders who are in it for the long haul, leaders who are truly bringing their authentic voice to the whole leadership game, are those who constantly ask the question. It's not so much about me. But does the organization, the team's goal get met in this collective endeavor? Many times, you know, of leaders who are playing these games and they are trying to strategize and they are trying to make these moves so that they look good, they kind of get better. They go for the rewards they get.

They go for glory, so to speak. Finding personal success is important. But if it is happening at the expense of the larger good, then you are not a great leader. You are not a successful leader for the long haul. So I would argue that right from the early days of pursuit of leadership, try and ask yourself what I'm doing. Is it in the interest of the larger goal, the collective goal, the common good of the organization? Only those who believe a premium on the collective good and the higher good will eventually get to prime positions of leadership. Otherwise, many of them just stay as individual achievers, never able to rally people behind them. You know, there's a saying that says if you want to go alone, you can go fast, but if you want to go far.

If you want to play this long whole game, then you need to take others with you, because when others are coming along and you see a sense of energy that you get from leading people to their dreams and to their aspirations, you are able to achieve a lot more for a long, sustained period of time. What sort of a leader do you want to become? You want to become this high, fast growth majority leader who just goes out in a blaze of glory? Or do you want to be a leader who is in it for a long time, who is willing to take people along with them and build their joys and dreams as you keep going along? Take a moment to reflect on what type of a leader you would like to become in the definition of common good.

Leadership Exacts A Price

Leadership exacts a price. Are you willing to pay the cost of leadership, the cost of leadership is your willingness to pay with your convictions. The cost of leadership is willingness to be courageous in the form of differing viewpoints. The ability to hold on to your core convictions is leadership. For example, when you come to a fork in the road or when your team needs to make a decision for yourself, the criteria that you use to make a decision is a function of your convictions. Are you willing to just go with the most expedient, the most convenient option, or do you stand for something so those convictions determine what you reflect as a leader and the convictions that drive you? Do you have the courage to stand for something? Leaders always, always stand for a set of beliefs or convictions that drive their choices.

Otherwise, they are referred to as spineless leaders or people who lead by consensus, who just ask around, vote, take a popular opinion and then just go ahead and make a decision. That's not the kind of leader you want to be. You want to be a leader who knows the beliefs and the convictions that drive you as an individual, the values that drive you as an individual and allows those to be reflected in your leadership style. What are the values that you stand for? Are you willing to take an unpopular stand when everyone around you is rooting for a particular book of action? That will set you up for leadership.

whether you are willing to be swayed by popular opinion or stand for what you believe is right for yourself, for the organization, for the customer, for the team that is involved in the decisions of all some of the principals that are at play. You know, often we have conflicts both for the actual issue and the circumstance itself. But sometimes you also have conflicts because of the principle behind the conflict. So how far are you willing to go into conflict for a belief or a principle that drives you? Take a moment to answer this question. How is your courage in the face of difficult choices and how far are you willing to go to take a stand even against popular belief?

Every Leader Begins With This Primordial Question - What Is My

At the heart of every leader is a personal Everist. You think of the greatest leaders that have left their imprint on the world, they are known to have found a personal Everist and they spent their entire life trying to get to the top of this Everest, their personal Everest. What's your Everest? What is this consuming dream that you have that is just keeping you obsessed every waking moment of your life? You know, many years ago when we were in England, we mentored one young girl and this young lady was so bubbly and so enthusiastic. Her entire life's dream was to become a weather reporter. I mean, I don't know if you meet too many people who ever say, I want to be a meteorologist. Right.

And this young girl's finger was then and she would just walk around with just say, you know, folks, today's weather forecast isn't. And they would all be just smiling at this enthusiasm of this young lady. And then I found the key to someone's personal Everest. What is it that keeps you up when you're not able to sleep in your bed, when you're tossing around and when you are restless, what consumes your mind is your personal Everest. What are some of the things that you are thinking or surfing when you're on the Internet? What are some of the things that you're constantly going and looking up that provide you the key, the clue to discovering your personal Everest? As a leader, you need to be driven by your personal Everest.

Whether it is success inside the corporate world or you're an entrepreneur, you're building a product. You want to go and get something done in your professional sphere, a degree, a high profile achievement, whatever is what is your personal success? Highest summit that will determine the time that your life is spent pursuing is your personal Everest. I want you to make a reflective, thoughtful response to this question. What is my personal Everest?

Leaders Pay Heed To Their Inner Voice

Another very important tool that every leader possesses is called the inner voice. Now. There is a point when all the data in the world. Will not be sufficient enough to make a decision at which point you have to make a leap of faith. What are you doing in NYC at those moments? There are times when you just are in a quandary. Not sure, because all the options seem to be legitimate and compelling enough. You don't know which way to go. What does your inner voice say in those moments, training your inner voice and listening to that inner voice is an important aspect of leaders. Great leaders have this intuition or a reflective tool that they've built over the years where they listen to all the viewpoints and eventually make their own decision based on what their inner voice is.

Sometimes it does go in addition to the line with which others have provided their input. And sometimes it goes contrary. But it is always because they listened to their inner voice. In today's day and age, people are not at all finding time to listen and pay heed to their inner voice. It's important that you are constantly shutting away from all these gadgets, devices and these voices that are coming at you to listen to what your own inner feelings in a way, says as to what is the right decision. Critical decisions, high stakes decisions need to be taken with the help of your inner voice. How good are you at using and listening to your inner voice?

There Is Difference Between Self-Awareness And Self-Delusion

The article at Delfi says, Know thyself, and in that principle, a leader tries a leader is firmly rooted in self-knowledge in the sense there's an uncanny understanding of the strengths that the leader possesses you possess as an individual. There's an uncanny understanding of the people around them in the sense of what their strengths are and how they can complement each other. But there's also another dimension to leadership, which is self-awareness, but there's also self-deception. Now, if you're not aware, then this leadership becomes this big delusion of grandeur, of this almost conceited notion that you are somehow better than others, as opposed to saying, these are my strengths that I bring to it for the benefit of ourselves.

Deception and self-delusion are two phrases that you ought to be extremely wary of, because that's where most leaders find themselves kind of trapped because they are not often aware of some of their own blind spots, so to speak. So what are some of these traps manifest themselves into? For example, one of the things that self-deception tends to do is to exaggerate one's own strengths and minimize the other's strengths. And it happens all the time in the corporate world during, let's say, an appraisal time, a season where bonuses are given or pay raises are given. You see a lot of hurting individuals because their leader did not recognize their contribution, their performance, their energy and their gifts and talents that they brought throughout the toiling and diligent manner.

Whereas the leader thinks it was me who was able to bring all of these people together and manage and so this notion of exaggerated opinions about oneself and diminished opinions about others is the conflict between self-awareness and self-delusion. Great leaders are aware of what gifts they bring. And also have an equally accurate understanding of the gifts and talents that others bring. How do you see yourself? Do you, you know, sort of rationalize everyone else's success but just justify and feel victimized about your own lack of success? I think that is a sign of self-deception. If you are able to look at somebody else's success and almost rationally explain their success, saying, hey, this could be because you deployed as gifts or gifts, it could be that they outworked me or they worked really hard as opposed to just attributing it to luck or favoritism or some kind of a very not so benevolent compliment. What are some of the blind spots that you struggle with in your own awareness of yourself as an individual?

Leadership Is A Self-Taught Path That Is Anchored In Reflection

How often do you wish that somebody just gave you a secret recipe for leadership, right? I wish somebody would give me one that would have allowed me to just avoid a lot of mistakes I made along the way. Leadership is self-taught. You have to be committed to be able to teach yourself on this journey of leadership and that this is not an exact science like let's say chemistry is where you just, you know, study the discipline, memorize the formula. And then after a while, you are seen as an expert. Leadership is a contact sport and the variables are as complex as the human beings and their behaviors and their emotions that are contained inside of them, because it is a people's game and because it is such a complex and unpredictable sort of an area. You have to be committed to teaching yourself every step along the way, just like you're taking this book. I wish 20 years ago someone told me to do some of what is being offered on a chapter book like this.

There wasn't a time in my life where I was not consuming material about leadership. There wasn't a time when I was not teaching myself the whole notion of how to be a leader in the future. So in that sense, it's a continuous, self taught process. If anyone says, oh, I have achieved, I mean, this great achievement, I'm done. I think that's where the backsliding will start. And then they are no longer in the coveted leadership position that they are and competition can just easily outmaneuver them. Leadership is a self-taught, ever evolving discipline where you are committed to reflecting on your own self and the team all the time.

So what might you take away from this? It means that you stay the book in this book, you stay till the end and grapple with some of the ideas that I'm presenting. It also means that you take copious notes. You used to engage with this material. You agree and you disagree and you challenge what I am doing and join a group of fellow students who are pursuing this subject matter expertise diligently. And then in the process of practicing what you are doing, either with a colleague or with someone else, you will find that many of these concepts are coming alive with the clarity that we would like to give to help us keep moving forward. Are you committed to teaching yourself for the rest of your life starting today?

Leaders Are Generators Of Tremendous Value - Followers Merely

As most adults, identity comes from creating stuff, generating stuff for accumulating stuff for ourselves, right? I mean, if you're wealthy, you have lots of money in the bank, then it kind of gives you confidence. If you have a bunch of cards as your possessions, then it gives you an identity, identity as to what you drive. If you have a lot of houses and homes and properties, that sort of you are seen as a kind of wealthy man who's achieved identity in adult life depends on whether you're creating new things for yourself or you are depleting things for yourself. It's a pretty obvious metric of success, but a leader's identity comes from generating value as opposed to diminishing value followers either protecting or preserving value. But leaders generate and create value.

If you are aspiring for leadership, your capacity to create value and create ideas, if you are in the ideas business or create products, if you are in the products business is a function of your leadership. You are measured by your capacity to create new ideas that will result in monetary value for your organization. Have you heard of performers in the world of sports or actors who deliver box office hits or if they don't, you are as good as your last success, right? You're as good as your last commercial success in some ways. And so with leadership too, it's no different. You are known for your last most valuable contribution that you made to your workplace if you are an entrepreneur. What was your last commercial success that you had? If you're a student, then academic success is what you should be gauging yourself by. So a leader's identity comes from being a generator of value, a generator of value, not a distributor or a prisoner of value, as followers are expected to do.

Intellectual Horsepower Is Key To The Drive Of A Leader

A major part of the leadership journey is actually intellectual, intellectual acumen or intellectual capacity. No matter what tone people use in the business world, in the corporate world is your ability for you to look at things they are as they are and identify the gaps, you know, because of the ambiguity that surrounds it, because of the uncertainty that surrounds our business world, are pressing dynamics at our day to day job. It's very important that your intellectual acumen is sharp as you embrace these leadership situations. Now, if you just strictly go by the books, what you've learned at the business school or what your others are telling you, you just are reacting.

But a major part of leadership is just having this ability to read the gaps to see where the puck is going to borrow. Wayne Gretzky is, of book, to be able to go to where the gaps are and identify the situation for your firm's competitive advantage or your team's advantage due to being able to look good by creating more value in the gaps. The ability to create value in the gaps comes from a very sharp inside of the strategy of the firm of technical knowledge, all those other criteria that add up to your intellectual acumen, if other things being common, this forceful personality or communication skills or the ability to lead by goals, other things are being common. It's a leader's intellectual acumen that sets him or her above the rest.

When it comes to reading situations, a strong intellectual acumen gives a tremendous situational intelligence to the ability to be able to read situations and advise their teams. And also it gives them the best advantage of often going against the grain and doing things against popular wisdom because the leader sees that the tides are changing. I mean, if we all know what happened in the covid-19 situation, what you used to think of as normal or business as usual has just changed overnight. And so it called for a new set of leadership skills of being able to lead in the blind, improvise as you keep going along. And the leaders who are trained are the ones who are uncomfortable in the ambiguity because they possess this knowledge of the gaps. So I just want to challenge you by asking this question. How do I boost my intellectual acumen when it comes to leadership?

On A Spectrum Between Doers And Dreamers, Where Do You Fall?

The higher you go on the leadership scale, the more a dreamer you ought to be. You know, in the early days of your job, it's OK to be a door and Florida and doing things as at the entry level of being a junior executive in the company. That's fine. But if you want to become a leader, your capacity to be a dreamer is imperative. If if you are able to constantly talk in what if scenarios, then you are able to innovate for your company, for your team, for your other people around you, whereas the doers are constantly doing things and they're just so focused on doing that, this visualizing other possibilities becomes a part of the leader's responsibility. Let me ask you, do you lean more towards the dreaming capacity of the leader's job or I'm much more comfortable just rolling up your sleeves and getting the job done? I would argue that a good leader is predominantly a dreamer.

You are visualizing what you can do to make your team look better, do better as you advance your company's mission in the marketplace. The Dreamers are constantly driven to learn from other fields as well. For example, Steve Jobs is known to have invented the Macintosh's forms, all that because he took a book in calligraphy and a liberal arts college. Now just imagine this dreamer just trying to draw from the world of calligraphy and apply it into the world of computing. The world has not been the same ever since. So the ability for dreamers to borrow from diverse sets of disciplines, from art, from music, from

from other skills, to put it in their context, sets them up to be amazing leaders. Are you a dreamer who is committed to learning all the time?

Leaders Never Hit Rock Bottom, They Use It As A Springboard To Bounce Back

Leaders are constantly learning from every conceivable source of travel. Friends and mentors, influencers, teachers, but their biggest source of learning is adversity. You know, I've been around in the corporate world for a long, long time. Everyone talks and pays lip service to we are a risk taking culture. We have an entrepreneurial culture and so on. But the first mistake somebody makes, they come down rapping on their knuckles and almost those two seem to contradict with each other. If a leader can learn a lot more from failure and adversity and setbacks, then when they hit the high marks and we hit the high bars, everything in the strategy comes together beautifully and they win in their quest for success. Leaders reflect on a lot of dynamics when things go wrong.

It forces the team to be humble. It forces the leader to just take a step back and think and analyze the root causes and reasons why they kind of fell apart. And what are the areas where they fell apart in their quest for success. So adversity actually makes a better picture than success as far as offering insights into the leadership behaviors concerned. Because when you get a set back, the true colors of the teams start emerging. The leaders show their true colors. It's all nice and warm and fuzzy when things are alright. But when he first set back his team leaders, true colors weren't so easy, as jovial and encouraging as he was before. Or is he falling apart because suddenly the spotlight is on him because of the perceived failure or a setback? So adversity offers tremendous amounts of learning and good leaders thrive learning from adversity. How good are you in your capacity to handle setbacks?

Leaders Thrive Or Melt Under Pressure

Someone defined grace under pressure is leadership. You know, it's easy to be a leader when there's no pressure. It's like child's play. Any child can be a leader and there is no pressure. But when the stakes are high, when there is a tremendous amount of reputation, tremendous amount of profit, tremendous amount of revenue, tremendous amount of relationships and capital that thrives on that hinges on the decisions you're making, that's pressure. And leadership is the ability to just navigate these thorny issues with grace and with calmness and with the preparedness of a seasoned performer, a musician or or a dancer or an actor who's just unfazed when the spotlight is shown on that person. You know, I've been an immature musician, and I'm occasionally prone to sort of riffing off here and there on my guitar.

You know, when you're playing in a band, suddenly the focus shifts on you when it's your time to solo. And the ones who are incredibly comfortable are those who have just practiced for that moment. But if you're not and I measure your fingers, start tightening, then you're a little fazed by the pressure that comes on you. And leadership is a bit like that. You have to have that grace and the ability to thrive under pressure, which will set you up for future success. But if you sort of cave in at that moment, then when you are at that moment, you are setting up for only learning because that's a set back moment. Leaders do not cave under pressure. They, in fact, thrive under pressure. It's called grace. You have to set yourself for high stakes relationships. You have to set up for high stakes where the objective that you are fighting for is so much, so much is riding on the outcome. Great leaders. Are graceful underpressure.

Singular Benefits Of Leadership

Imagine living the life of your dreams. Leadership makes it possible. Imagine setting high standards for yourself as far as your success goals are concerned, going out and achieving them. This leadership book will set you up on that journey to get what you dream and set goals for imagined, working with people and rallying them around for a common cause. This leadership book will allow you to go out there, get the design and the destiny of your life, and in the process impact others as well through your leadership skills. Leadership is all about leading first for yourself and others due to everyone's mutual success. And this leadership book is all about that.

How do you identify your dreams, your desires, and then set milestones with discipline, with the diligence that is needed to go out and achieve them? This, of book, has nothing but the promise to make your potential come alive in the process, transforming yourself and transforming scores of lives around you, because that's what great leaders do if they go get a life of their dreams. But in the process, they also inspire and impact everyone around them. If this encourages you to stay with us and see you on the summit of success.

Leadership Is Both Substance And Style

At the end of every chapter, you should be asking this question. Is this idea advancing the substance of my leadership or the style, the outward manifestation of the leadership? There are two components to every element in the leadership journey, form and function, style and substance, content and intent. How you manifest in these two areas will really determine what sort of leader you are. Now, in this world, there are different types of leaders, some who are very flamboyant, very charismatic, very vivid, some in the way the optics are presented, see all the right things. Yet there is an element about them that is the believability and the trustability and the trustworthiness that that affects them.

So during your leadership journey, you need to ask yourself this question, where does this chapter fall and does it fall in the substance element or does it fall in the style element? Am I working on the outworking or am I working on the inner workings of the behavior, the attitude, the mindset element? So those two elements, if you are able to navigate on your leadership journey, then you are making progress because ultimately you cannot have anything that is stylistically marvelous yet struggle on the substance level. And yet, if you have the greatest character and the greatest substance in the world, but you are not making an impact from a state standpoint, then you would still be struggling. So no matter which way, at the end of every chapter asked this question, is it enhancing my substance or style? Is it about the structure and the intent and the optics that that goes outside or it is about the content and my deep behavioral related choices that I'm making.

Leadership Is Built On These Two Principles Of Physics

Let me introduce to you two quick principles of physics for your learning journey. The first one is motion. I want you to start looking at each chapter as adding motion to your growth journey. Take a moment. And as you go past each chapter, pause and ask yourself, what is it that I'm getting out of this chapter that's motion for you. But the second one I really want you to pay attention to, in addition to motion, is momentum. Momentum is the increase in the speed with which you are learning and applying things for yourself. So motion will allow you to explore every idea that comes in hits your mind, but it's the momentum that actually takes you further.

How might that allow me to apply it in my setting? How might that help me make changes to my current thinking? How might that idea that I just heard impact the goals and the vision for my future? So if you are able to start asking these questions after every chapter, then the power of motion and the power of momentum will come together and help you. So always remember you will not be able to get momentum without the motion. But after a few chapters, if you're not getting the momentum, then which means you are not really applying yourself to saying what's in it for me, how can I apply some of this teacher's teaching to my setting? So try and see if we can bring both emotion and momentum into your learning journey. The adventure will become an exciting roller coaster for you.

It Is Never About Being A Superhero, In Reality

The second element that you should always remember is in addition to the winner at every cost, win everything at any cost kind of a thing is to also make sure that you don't project yourself as a superhero. Invincible, indefeasible, undefeatable, indefatigable leadership is never in the realm of fantasy. It's in the realm of reality. So if you are a real, authentic leader, you will refrain from projecting this, Oh, I'm a superhero, I, I don't have any eckles. He has a kind of mindset. True leadership is about being genuine to the core of being vulnerable to your dreams, of being courageous in the face of fears, of being authentic and even in testing times. That's what teams look for in you. And if you're afraid to show your human side, but you're just hiding behind a title and a glass door and a and and an artificially built up image, then you're not being authentic. So the second element that you want to refrain from is projecting this aura of this superhero stay real grounded in reality.

It's About Not Being Blindsided

Have you ever heard the term blind spot of a leader? Well, every leader has them. I have them, too. But what is important is that if we start with the assumption that you will have blind spots, then you will build ways, mechanisms, counterweights that will allow you to still overcome some of the issues that might spring from having a blind blind spot. You have to have good mentors, good team members who can speak truth to power in your condition so that you are aware of any crisis that might come out of a blind spot. I've built off a bunch of blind spots that every leader might fall prey to. And here's one of them. The most notable one was to think that winning is everything. Winning is everything and winning at any cost. Leadership is about knowing that there are a few important goals to go after, vitally important goals to go after.

And then there are some that even if you don't win them, it's fine to. But by not exerting pressure on winning everything, they release themselves from the pressure to win everything at any cost versus winning on the critical few that make a difference. It also allows your team members to relax a bit from those that pressure to win everything at all costs that win everything at all costs does exert. It costs a price on the health, mental health and the resources of the people around you. So one of the first Blancs part is to win everything at any cost. That is a big trap that you want to stay away from.

Leadership Is About Solving The Gaps

Here's a quick one for you. Any time you hear leadership, here's a four letter acronym that will allow you to capture anything about leadership. It's one of the most simplistic definitions I've heard. It worked for me very well. So I'm sure it's the word gaps that the G in Gap stands for your goals. What are the goals? What do you like to achieve? What are your aspirations? What are your dreams? How do you want to go about achieving those goals? The second element is your abilities. Do you possess the necessary elements to go to your goals or like the scores you're taking in the hope to improve and expand your abilities? If you have them, you're already building on them, or if you don't, you're acquiring those abilities. So goals, abilities.

The B is about perceptions. What do others see about you and what do you see for yourself? What do you possess that self perception that you are out to achieve? You are a conqueror. You're a champion. You have this positive mindset. It's all about perception and it is for the standards and strategies that others will expect from you. So goals, abilities, perception and strategies and standards. So put it together. Then you have a definition of leadership that will allow you to go to any situation and apply these four letters and have a view, a tool to decipher what's going on.

Let's say you join a new team, apply the GOP's principle. You have a goal to succeed in the new team. Then you also have the abilities or you have to build the abilities needed to succeed.

Then there are issues about perception. How does the team perceive you? How do you perceive the team? Then the whole perception plays out. And finally, standards and strategies to make it come through in that team. So no matter where your situation is, you can apply this Gap's principle to get into your leadership situation.

It Affects Your Whole Person, This Leadership Quest

Two broad dimensions in which leadership can manifest itself. One is your personal life and the other is your professional or business life. Now, if you unshackle the left's self limiting beliefs and you start expanding your own mental limits, then you have set for yourself. Group triggers ability for you to impact your immediate circle of family and friends and the community you live in. And the other side is the professional growth that may happen because of the excellence that you bring at work, because of your constant drive to improve yourself. No, sometimes you cannot achieve professional success until you start seeing results in your personal life.

So no matter what situation you are an entry level leadership or you're already a little bit of an experienced professional, no matter where you are, you ought to commit yourself to personal growth where you start seeing the limits for yourself and as well as succeeding professionally. Only these two come together. You will see a lot of fulfillment, a lot of happiness in your own life. So right now, stop and start thinking, what are some of the top two goals that I need to set for myself in my personal life as well as professional life?

You Could Be The Biggest Barrier To Your Growth

Here's a quick one for you. One of the big limits to learning anything is the barriers that you impose on yourself, some preconceived notions. Let me ask you, what are some of the preconceived notions that you might have that will help you from getting the full benefits of this book?

The fact is that You are looking at it with skepticism and cynicism stop you from your journey, does the fact that you come and say, I want to judge this person on the basis of how the of the facilitator looks or his credentials, do not you got to examine each idea for what it is, what not the messenger.

The message for you is very important. So stop everything right now and empty yourself from all the preconceived notions that might hinder your getting value from the book. Do not let anything that might take away the sheen from the power of these ideas. Let the validity of the idea, let the power of the idea speak to you and pay attention to the barriers that may diminish the value of a book for you. Do not be cynical. Do not let any negative feelings stop you from getting the full benefits from this book.

There Is No I In Leader

Another common refrain that U.S. leaders use is the word I so much so that we can call them ICE specialists. I personally have worked in the corporate world and the business world. And every time I hear leaders talk about the team in the first person singular, then I start cringing leaders or to be inclusive by definition.

And the word I should only be used almost sparingly and constantly have communication around them and include everyone in the room. The ability for a leader to understand the power of each word he speaks is so crucial to the overall morale, the energy and the vibe of the team.

So stop being an eye specialist. Focus on the team, focus on the challenge, focus on what's in it for the others around you. And sometimes, yes, it is the ego that sets up the leader for all the challenges that are out there to be surmounted. But when it is coming out of their mouth, the world ought to be about the team and we the world we should be taking more precedence over I.

Have You Ever Thought About When It Is A Good Time To Grow As A Leader?

So when is a good time to commit to leadership development, someone said the best time to plant a tree was yesterday. The second best time, however, is today. So today is the day you should be committing yourself to improve yourself, to expand your horizons, to to develop the potential that is inside of you for greatness. For success. Unless you do something today, it won't make a difference for your tomorrow. You can't undo what happened yesterday. There's nothing unless you can reflect and learn some chapters out of it. You won't be able to control what happened yesterday. But what you can control is what you can do today to commit yourself to this journey of improving yourself. What you won't be able to do anything about is for tomorrow.

Do not postpone stuff for tomorrow, because tomorrow, you know, don't know what priorities and pressures you might face. So what you can actually do is now that you're here noodling around on you. To me, this is a chance for you to commit to a journey that will impact your future, your near-term future, your long term future. So no matter what your goal is to pursue, you have to pursue wealth, to pursue success, to seek to go and become an entrepreneur, whatever might be the larger goal. The only way you can impact your future is taking urgent action today.

Leadership Is Never About One Definitive Answer

A common trap that leaders fall into is to believe that there is only one style of functioning or only one way of skinning the cat, which might be their way of doing it. So their default state, their dominant style, often becomes their golden style instead of being an adaptive leader who calls for different types of behaviors under different circumstances. For example, if they achieve this aggressive goal, getting a high energy type of a leader, if they apply that even to a crisis situation, the crisis situation will just flare up into a bigger crisis. But crisis situations call for a more calm, more composed, more mature sort of response than the dominant default aggressive let's call move things, shake off the trees kind of mindset.

And on the other hand, this calm, composed mindset which works very well, you know, you know, in a situation that demands such a style will not work where there is a sense of urgency, there is a quarter quarterly deadline looming and you've got to marshal all the forces, all the people to to rally into them into an almost like of going to war type of an energy that still won't work here. So a true leader understands that there are different stages of response called under different sets of conditions and draws them accordingly and marches to the dictates of that situation.

Leadership Is Launching Into The Unknown

Here's another challenge for you, leadership is always about embracing the unknown. You assume a set of assumptions and parameters that you base your plan on, and as you launch into the unknown, you will start discovering that those assumptions are either playing out or not playing out. But the element of unknown is what propels the leader.

As you embark on this book, I want to ask you, how comfortable are you with this element? Unknown, because this book promises to be rich, insightful and offer you many insights that can propel you in your own leadership journey. But how comfortable you are with this unknown element determines your readiness to embrace these ideas and notions so taken from me, this ability to embrace the unknown will set you up as a leader. In my own case, I'm always excited by the unknown as opposed to being innovated or exhausted by the unknown.

So take a moment to ask yourself, am I excited by the unknown or does that prospect of the unknown scare me? Take a moment to reflect on this as well.

U Don't Jump The Seas In One Big Leap

Here's another quick one for you. Do not think of success as trying to reach the top of a staircase. Think of it as what might be the next one step that I might take as I try and get to the staircase, no matter what you use as a metaphor, whether it's a staircase to the top on a ladder to the top of the pyramid that you are climbing to get to the top or even a marathon journey, you can never at one quantum leap get to the end zone. You will always have to take one step, gain an inch to borrow a sports metaphor. You gain an inch before you get to the yards, right? So it's always what you did today.

And what will be the incremental one benefit that you can get out of this book that will help you get moving forward? Very important. If you want to make great gains in your growth, you don't have to think big, huge transformational jumps or leaps. You need to say, what is the one little habit that I can tweak? One little choice that I might take one one, one little step in the right direction that will help me keep going forward. So always remember, don't think about the entire staircase. Think of one step at a time.

Leadership Is Built On The Bedrock Of Confidence

Assume a word that is normally associated with leaders is confidence. No confidence again stems from your previous track record of having realistic, verifiable proof that you crossed such bridges before and therefore using that knowledge that you are able to be secure, that you can solve any problem again in the future.

Leaders are confident. People who enjoy being around others, then they are never insecure. They never get threatened by other leaders because they know that the security comes from their own ability to resolve problems without necessarily falling apart.

And it is this set of leaders who are confident that bring the best out of others, because when a leader is calm, composed and is aware of his own internal locus. Then people around him feel confident that they, too, can overcome any problem. Take a moment to ask yourself how confident are you as a leader?

Is There Anything New Under The Sun?

Have you heard the phrase old wine in a new bottle? To me, that phrase actually captures the essence of all leadership principles. There is no new principle that will capture your attention other than something that is contextualized for our times. That is ancient classical wisdom that philosophers have just kept passing it down through the ages. But there are also these brilliant thinkers who take ancient ideas or classical ideas and contextualize it to our times.

The wisdom that you can get out of this is how do I apply it to my situation? How do I apply in my context? It is that ability to know what you can take from each chapter, each chapter, and apply to your situation that allows you to get the very best out of the scores. You can transform your world if you grapple with all the notions that book has to offer.

On the other hand, you could also get cynical and say, and it really is a lot of hard work because leadership is not and it's not for the faint hearted. Leadership, by definition means that you are trying to capture and capture the imagination of people and harness their emotions and bring them along with you on this exciting path called success. But if you're not excited, if you're not enthused, if you are not willing to put in the hard yards, then maybe leadership is not for you.

You might just be content going along as a follower or just play along in a team that requires others to step up to the leadership role. But true leadership is always about saying, I'm energized, I'm enthused. Let me take these ideas and apply them in my context.

Leadership Is The Sum Total Of The Problems Solved

Your leadership journey is actually a sum total of the problems you solved. You know, have you ever wondered why people get promoted at the workplace or in the corporate world? It is because they have demonstrated that they are capable of solving problems in their previous roles, in their previous capacities. And that track record will set them up for the unknown of the future roles where they will solve bigger, more complex problems.

So this dimension of problem solving is an important aspect of leadership, whether it is people, complex, people, related problems, which involves change management, organizational behavior and so on and so forth, or customer problems where you're solving a pressing problem for a customer or if you are in the world of finance, it's related to capital deployment and so on and so forth.

No matter what you're doing, the common theme that runs in all of this is your capacity for problem solving. If you enjoy solving problems, then you are cut out to be a leader, your growth and your augmented capacity will set you up for more problem solving in the future. How good are you at solving problems?

Explore These Ideas For The Fundamentals Of Leadership

The Seven Ps of Leadership – Foundations of your Leadership Structure Purpose Discovering the Why and What of your calling. Why is it important for you to become a leader? What benefits might you receive when you get to be a leader?

People Uncovering the felt and unfelt needs of folks around u Priorities What are the combined goals of you and your team/unit/business that are being accomplished Performance How do you know when you are successful? What does success look like? Planning How are you realizing your goals? What actions, choices are to be made from a resources and timing perspective?

Persistence When you don't succeed first, what are your alternate books of action? How often can you repeat your actions for success? Provision What resources, personnel and tools can be provided to your team to make them successful.

Leadership Is Growth - Are You Prepared For The Growth Pangs

There are more than 10000 thousand books on Google. If you just search for leadership. But to me, the most meaningful definition of leadership is growth. Leadership is growth. Have you ever wondered why growth is such an inescapable part of life? B When a child is growing, we always associate them with the appropriate milestones expected at a particular point in time. At five years, you expect them to have certain milestones. Likewise, in a leadership journey. A person is only growing in direct. Proportion to their leadership skill development, if they are growing, if their knowledge is growing, if their insights are growing, then they are making progress and strides in leadership.

Unfortunately, whether it's in the corporate world or in the world of academia or in the world of nonprofits, we are always seeing leaders plateau. We see leaders stagnate at a certain level. And that, my friend, is the opposite of growth. It is decay, it is entropy, it is stagnation. And so here's my challenge for you. Are you committed to this leadership journey where you are committed indirectly, directly to your growth? Take a moment to reflect on that.

Leaders Are A Series Of Decisions - Good And Bad

How do you make good decisions by making a series of bad decisions, right? I mean, I might sound flippant, but judgment in a leader comes from a series of mistakes and erroneous decisions taken in the past. Seasoned judgment comes from making multiple decisions over us over a set period of time in the leadership journey. Now, if you're smart.

Seasoned judgment is used when you are able to draw from all your past decision making criteria and apply that to the current situation. Data is important. Various scenarios are important in the scenario, planning is important, but ultimately the judgment and a decision that needs to leap off from data comes down to an individual's judgment and decision making capability.

Leadership is about seasoned judgment. Leadership is about taking intuitive calls about the decision that you are making. How good are you at making decisions when data is not sufficient, but it's not fully complete. Your ability to decide comes in. So leaders display excellent judgment.

Leadership Is A Choice

Leadership is a choice, in fact, right now you have a choice to stay on and persist with this book or just get distracted into something else and do your own old habits or some other stuff. This choice alone will set up for a better destiny. This choice alone will help you in the future. Just this choice alone, if embraced wholeheartedly, can set you up on a path to prosperity, peace and success.

Four Benefits From This Book

I'd like to offer you four benefits as to why you should take this book, the first one being it would give you immense self-confidence. That we have just two decades of professional and corporate and entrepreneurial experience to sort of. He offered as condensed wisdom should give you a tremendous confidence to just apply it and see it come alive. The second one is the tremendous rewards that you might get as a result of promotion or a higher responsibility at work because of the confidence that you've already built because of this book. So the rewards could be many. The third one is the outcome of this book could result in excellence, both at work or in your personal life, that you start setting higher standards and start living up to lofty standards.

So excellence can also be a big benefit as a result of this book. And finally, when applied, all these concepts, tools, techniques, stories and all the energy that you receive from the scores can result in heightened performance at work or rekindle your passion as an entrepreneur or whatever sphere of life you're in. It will definitely augment or amplify your performance. So if you are ready to make some radical changes in your life. Still grappling with these ideas, and I am sure we will see you on the other side of success.

Why Is This Book Different

Let me answer this question, why is this cause better than any leadership book that's out there? But first of all, this leadership book is taught by a practitioner, someone who's walked the walk and talks, the talk, so to speak, over three decades of corporate and field experience, distilled into manageable short insights laced with great personal stories. So there you are. The first advantage is that it's a very practical book. I wouldn't share something that I have not practiced, not found in empirical evidence. The second benefit is because of what has happened in the world of management, in the world of technology, in the world of corporate, global, corporate entities, I bring the latest insights that we are seeing as management insights.

So you're really getting what is out there, not some dry academic research, but seen on the field as practitioners we run into and so on and so forth. The third and final benefit that you would get again out of this is if applied, some of these concepts can straightaway start delivering great results for you in your life. Why? Because my own journey came from this bootstrapping and self development committed to a lifetime of learning. So there you are, it's practical, it resonates with the corporate world out there, and more importantly, it stems from a personal journey that I committed to a lifetime of learning and based on my own story. It should be evident to you that if it weren't for him, there's a good chance that this will work for me.

I was not even given a chance to survive. Forget about coming into the corporate world or having a job. I was going to be written off as a criminal, a hoodlum hooligan. But my story turned around and I had committed myself to a great time of learning and self-improvement, which set me up on this love of leadership. So there you are. It works. It's been proven. It has repeatability. I've impacted thousands of people already and I'm sure this book will impact you and transform you. So give it a shot and watch magic happen.

You Can Run On Yesterday's Diet

Here's a quick one for you. You cannot win today's and tomorrow's battles with yesterday's skills. What do I mean by that, you want to upgrade your knowledge, you want to upgrade your skills, you want to be on what is called the cutting edge of leadership.

Why? Because the context and the times and the circumstances of business have changed, everything has become digital, everything has become almost the center of customer experience has now become digital, which means you have to, as a leader, adapt to new technologies, new ideas out there in the marketplace.

So that's why you need to embrace a book like this and grapple with the concepts that we are trying to offer. Filter through decades of experience. We are trying to bring the scores to your advantage so that you don't have to reinvent the wheel, but embrace this, grapple with this and contextualize this to yourself.

Leadership Myths - No One Is Born A Leader

There is this notion that leaders are born into a genetic pool and then you are born together and you stay a leader and so on and so forth. But nothing could be further from the truth. True leaders evolve over a period of time in different settings and different situations, so that's a myth that needs to be debunked. Leaders do not become leaders because of a genetic lottery or they are born with certain skills and traits. Yes, some of these traits are natural. And then we talk about natural strengths and gifts and talents. But to believe that a leader on the whole is born because of a genetic selection is a big myth. So that's a takeaway for you. You are not born a leader.

True leaders are proven in different contexts and different settings, and they prove themselves with their choices, with their behaviors, with the communication and. Finally, performance in those settings, so it's a myth to think that, oh, no, I'm not a born leader. No, you can always start the leadership journey and embark and develop yourself and bootstrap yourself into becoming a leader. Take my own example. I was never destined to be a leader if it were not for a mysterious turn of events that led me on to the journey of becoming a leader. So two or three decades later, I am now at a point where I'm teaching leadership. So if I could do it, anybody can do it.

Leaders Are Not Made Based On Degree Or Pedigree

Another myth that surrounds leadership is that they have to have these high degrees and a high amount of education in order to be excellent leaders. The truth is far from it. Education gives you some degree of to some degree of concepts, conceptual frameworks and ideas, but it's actually the sum total of your skills, strengths and talents and behaviors demonstrated over a period of time that makes a leader, a leader like this. Great education gets you in the door. But what you deliver inside, in the stadium, in the hard knocks in the marketplace is actually what sets you up as a leader. If education alone were the criteria for good leaders, I would have never had a chance to become a leader because there are more educated people in this world, more MBAs from different schools of pedigree and so on.

But it's not what an MBA degree that gives you the leadership skills, the leadership skills that you acquired over a period of time. And how you deploy those skills over a period of time sets you up to be a great leader. So if you're one of those who are struggling and say, Hmm, I don't have an MBA degree, I don't have this great Ivy League pedigree type of education degree. Do not fret, be encouraged, if I could compete in the corporate place, if I could travel as an immigrant, if I could do all this. Believe me, you can do it, too. And if given an opportunity, if you could just demonstrate how you could evolve as a leader by taking this book, by proving yourself in many settings, nothing can stop you. The world belongs to those who believe in the power of their dreams. Do not let the lack of education or lack of a big degree stop you and limit you in pursuing your destiny. Your destiny is far higher than a degree, so go for it. Do not ever believe this myth that great leaders have to have great education.

Leadership Myths - They Don't Always Have To Be Charismatic

Another myth that people struggle with and believe is that Karisma is a big part of leadership and it's only the charismatic that become great leaders, like all these phenomenal leaders that we talk about, Martin Luther King, Nelson Mandela, Mahatma Gandhi, and ensure great leaders have charisma. But it is not entirely charisma that makes a great leader. What makes a great leader or someone who is a leader is real skills burnished over a period of time. What makes a great leader is drill management and people management skills that have been demonstrated amidst conflict, amidst turbulent times in difficult circumstances. And that's why they become leaders.

So this myth that. You've got to have this flamboyance about yourself that you have to have this absolutely gorgeous, charismatic personality to be a leader is another myth that needs to be slim. You need to be yourself. You can be whatever you are, the way you look, the way you behave, the way you make choices. That's the way you were designed, created. And then you do not have to be apologetic about the way you are and wish that you were somebody else. You can be who you are and still become a leader in your own right.

A Great Leader Does Not Have To Manipulate People Around

Another myth that people often think is leadership or management is always about manipulating people. Far from it, it's never about manipulating people. True leaders are true leadership is all about authenticity, all about being genuine at the core of your being. It's about leading by influence. I don't know whether I'd be using the word influence a lot, because if I can't appeal to the lead team members and followers and find what is in their genuine interest. That's what makes me a leader. If I can just bring the combined energies of the team members and harness them to pursue a common team goal or the organization goal, that's all leadership is.

Where people fall and there are some people who lend credence to this kind of myth is because they start thinking of winning at the expense of beating others, winning at the expense of manipulating and dominating others. Those leaders make this myth come alive. That winning is all about manipulating people and taking advantage of these gullible people. True leaders never manipulate their team's true leaders, never manipulate those who report to them. True leaders never, ever share information partially and hide information to take competitive advantage. Yes, there are times when you need to withhold information on a need to know basis.

But genuine leaders, for the most part, can never be accused of withholding information only except for personal gains. I have always tried to be an authentic leader who leads my influence, and that's why you need to just demolish this myth that there are these leaders who make you believe that this is indeed true, that true leadership is all about manipulation. No, it's always about influence.

Leaders Are Not Managers

Here's another quick one for you. Have you ever wondered what's the difference between a manager and a leader? People manage things or people manage resources, but they leave people. They lead people, so if you ever are thinking of a role as a manager, you are just looking at managing the resources, optimizing them, taking good customer custody of things that aren't you being a good custodian of finances, of human resources and stuff, you are merely looking at a manager role.

But if you want to grow in leadership, then it comes down to leading people, understanding what makes people tick, understanding the complexities of human behavior, human feelings, human emotions. And then. Galvanizing all those complex forces into effective performance, that is the difference between being a manager and a leader.

A Must Possess Quality For The Future, To Shine In The Business World

Here's a quick win for you. According to the World Economic Forum and among all the critical skills they're identified to succeed in the future, active learning and learning strategies is the second highest skill, most in demand in the next five seven years into the coming decade. The reason? Active learning and learning strategies become a key component of your own growth because of the rapid obsolescence of ideas, practices and notions and models that are in the business world. And as life around us goes into this swirling change, the ability for anyone to constantly evolve along with changing times is an integral part of their own personal growth.

So if I came to become what I have become over the period of 10, 15 years, then all that I've learned needs to be re-examined. And whatever doesn't work needs to be discarded. And a fresh set of ideas need to come in. So it comes down to a person's individual commitment to a lifetime of learning. And these learning skills, learning to learn becomes like this mental learning skill, so to speak, a skill of learning to learn, it becomes this all too important, critical success factor in your professional journey. You will never be able to succeed at business in the business world or the corporate world if you do not have an active learning strategy in place.

Which is why taking this book might be one of the best things that you've done. Because if you are able to just embrace all these notions that I am outlining for you, then you set for yourself a personal development plan, a learning plan for the next five years or so. And then you can review where you live, how far you've come, and then again, do another rain check and another rain strategy. So here's how the act of learning and your learning strategies will set you up for future success. And in the absence of which, you are only bound to make incremental progress, not exponential leaps. Take a moment to reflect on how your learning strategy is.

Another Must-Have Trait For The Future Leader

Another top skill in demand for the future from an employability point of view or for success as you embrace this leadership book is called leadership and social influence. You know, often leadership is seen as in a vacuum, but leadership's functionality and effectiveness comes only when it has social impact in that if you are able to leave yourself. That's great. But if you are able to influence a team which is social, then you are seen as a person who can make a difference to the world out there. So social influence becomes a decisive barometer in measuring your leadership success. And for some people, you can see that spark very early in life, right, in their high school days or middle school days, they can start seeing those glimpses of potential right there.

But it is only after a sustained period of time that you can say this person has struck true to form and lived out his potential. And that potential is manifested in social influence. The degree of leadership stature, the higher you go in the corporate world or in the business world, your influence is directly measured by social influence, the ability for you to build a talented team of people around you, the ability to manage them, the ability to build great products with them, the ability to take that products to market, the ability to monetize, the ability to raise and create profits. All of that actually translates to social influence as well.

So in addition to leadership and self-learning and learning strategies, leadership and social influence is another high. Desirable, much wanted skill for the future. So if you're taking this book, I would like you to sort of grapple with it on a day to day basis and really let the school speak to you, let the concepts sink into you to make a difference, to affect your thinking and to affect your feelings so that there is transformation inside out for a long time. You can never truly become a true leader if you do not increase your social influence.

A Leader Knows The Difference Between A Critic And A Coach

The difference between a good leader and a bad leader is a bad leader, a critic, a good leader is a coach. Now, that doesn't mean coaches don't critique. The spelling is different critique performance and don't offer insights on how to raise the bar and achieve more, they do, but they do it in a very constructive manner. By diffusing the emotion from the issue of performance, they attack the issues that are around performance, but they never attack the person that is for a bad leader. The issue and the person on the same, they just critique without necessarily building into it a component of constructive elements into it.

What sort of a person are you? Do you find it easy to be a critic? Do you find it easy to stay? Yeah, but. You know, there is always something negative that follows after the war, but. Instead, try to use the word yes and and offer your critique, then you are taking the role of a coach and then you are offering your analysis of what went wrong. Do not be a critic, but instead try and aspire to be a coach if you want to be a great leader.

An Inspiring Leader Is Also Unreasonable

Here's another quick tip for you: be unreasonable, be outrageous. What do I mean by that, the reasonable ones blend into the world and then just get by, it's the unreasonable, it's the outrageous, it's the audacious ones that go on and make a name for themselves. So let me ask you, are you unreasonable, audacious, ambitious as far as your aspirations are concerned?

If not, you need to be, because if you are blending in, trying to be the average and just be a part of the crowd, then leadership is not exactly the kind of skill that you should be looking for.

But if you want to be unreasonable, expect great things from yourself and those from around you. Then you are set up to be a New Age leader who not only expects great things from himself, but also pushes everyone around to attain great stuff.

A Good Leader Is Bold Not A Bully

Here's a quick one for you. The challenge and the clarion call for a leader is to be bold, to be audacious, to take great risks depending on the aspirations. But here's something that you should not be.

Do not be a bully. Often you see a lot of people who buy strength of their personality by strength of the title, by strength of their influence in the company are just downright bullies. Leaders can never be police leaders should not tolerate police, any form of intimidation or any form of sexual harassment should not be tolerated. So people don't bully.

The fine line is if people are feeling uncomfortable with your leadership, you are likely to be a bully, not a board leader.

This Leader Runs From Cheating - Self

One of the biggest forms of deception happens when you deceive yourself. Leaders always work towards minimizing self deception. What do I mean by self-deception when you know that you have to do the right thing but somehow find ways of justifying it and not do it? That's deception right there. Knowing to do the right thing and not doing it is deception. So leaders have to constantly minimize their knowledge between saying something in public as the right thing and not doing it. If there is a gap, then in simple words, it's called hypocrisy. These hypocritical leaders practice deception because they sort of justify under any circumstances why what they did or did not do was acceptable.

Ruthlessly honest leaders practice that self-awareness, and they are always willing to challenge themselves and say no, if it is not right, I'm not going to do it. Now, the words the corporate world is full of leaders will have failed and have fallen and have fallen from grace because of that lack of prudence, lack of ability to do the right thing at the right time, all the time. What sort of a person are you willing to cut corners when no one's watching? Are you willing to sort of pass off what is acceptable as acceptable when, you know, you could even do better than what has been done? Take a moment to ask yourself in this area of self deception, how am I if you think you're good enough, then maybe you are guilty of this, because leaders know that they are a work in progress.

They're always under construction. The road to leadership is under construction. And if you recognize that paradigm that we all work in progress, then you're constantly pushing the boundaries to get better. In fact, if you're taking this book, you recognize that you need all these training, all these skills and all these leadership development programs so that you can incorporate them into your life and become a better influential leader. So when it comes to self deception, be ruthless with yourself.

A Good Leader Knows The Difference Between A Learned Man And Learner

Here's another quick one for you. Do you want to be a learned man or a learner? The learned man is perfectly suited for an opportunity that doesn't exist, whereas a learner is constantly positioning himself for the opportunities that are coming in a dynamic way in front of him.

The little one, they seem to know it all. They seem to have all the answers. They are those who look at reality and have great theories to explain them. But the learner is constantly going about adapting himself to the new world order, to the changing things and riding the waves of opportunity.

Which one do you want to be? The loved one who can explain away everything to the learner, who can go and achieve anything?

A Fine Leader Knows The Opposite Of A Desire

Here's another quick one for you. Leaders are disciplined. But the opposite of a desire to pursue something is not the lack of desire, it is actually a denial of something else. Other things being equal, your designer should be strong, but your denial also should be equally strong.

Once you choose something, you're heading in that direction, but there are many distractions that you need to deny yourself to, and the stronger the capacity for denial, the greater the capacity to move in the direction of your desire. Ultimately, discipline is just the management of desire and denial.

The more you go towards desire, the more you have to also deny a whole lot of other things. In business parlance, it's called the opportunity cost, the price you pay or the price of a choice not taken or the road not taken. In simple terms, the stronger your capacity for denial, the greater ability to pursue your desire.

The Pandemic Leveled The Playing Field

The pandemic in many ways leveled the playing field for leaders again. What do I mean by leveling the playing field again? You know, back in the day, it used to be an advantage for people to be close to their bosses by constantly sort of doing things and ingratiating themselves.

And people who are not comfortable doing those kinds of things would be at a disadvantage. But now, with everything going virtual and to a foreseeable future, a large dependence on virtual kind of connections, you are at a disadvantage in that the rules are being set all over again. For example, If you want to demonstrate that you are capable of something now, what is happening is because almost everybody else is also watching on a call what you're potentially capable of, you are able to sort of perform in front of a gallery, which means that that exclusive back door office access that your colleagues used to try and get to with your boss and so on are now sort of minimized because it's a virtual playing field. So when your convictions are strong.

Do you sort of stay strong even when under attack from others or even when your bosses and others are trying to question or do you wilt under the criticism and sort of give up? You know, I had a boss who was constantly sort of challenging what I did, and he was trying to rip holes into whatever I was proposing. In fact, I used to do that even in front of a group. Then I said, what is the point of running these chapters by you and you've seen this and you OK, that I should present this and now you're asking the questions again, and I had to confront them in public. And because I did that once or twice, he stopped kind of embarrassing me in public, but the bickering and the continuous negativity continued even after a while.

So I had to call it out because at some point it started affecting me, even in terms of my mental health and how I was seen by others in the team. Toxic bosses have favorites, they love certain conversations to happen privately and in public, they play a different song or play a different tune. Your ability to shine gets tested when your convictions are held under any circumstances. How do you hold your convictions? Renaissance leaders are all about convictions. And even in the face of criticism, they don't vote, but they stay strong. They don't play safe. They are these swashbuckling types of leaders who are willing to defend their beliefs at any cost. You know, the world doesn't reward safe players, the world rewards those who are willing to take a stance and live by that stance and build a track record supporting that stance. How good are you when it comes to defending your convictions? Take a moment and reflect on a time where your convictions were tested and how did you come out of that experience?

In The Beginning, There Was A Leader Who Said" Let There Be Light"

Hey, folks, welcome back. In this chapter, I want to evaluate and introduce to you the seven PS of leadership, seven PS of leadership. The first element of the first B in this leadership is my purpose. In fact, the word purpose has now just become completely synonymous with Simon Sinek, who asked the question why of everything. Before you get to anything, you've got to know the why of something. In my view, the word purpose is. So powerful, so invigorating, so liberating, so direct that I would actually spend hours just talking about purpose, my own purpose, how I discovered my purpose and so on and so forth. But it's very important to know why you are on this leadership journey, is it to get better? Is it to secure that dream job? Is it to become healthy? Is it to become an entrepreneur? What's your driving factor? What's the biggest? Rationale, biggest motive, biggest intent as to why you want to be a leader.

Because if you can understand why, then everything else sort of falls into place, you know, when you were there, when you were young and when you are doing a puzzle or when you are doing Tetris, I remember just one block when you click that or when you have that, suddenly a whole lot of other blocks just fall into place. Purpose is a bit like that. Purpose is like that one block that can open multiple avenues for you in your leadership journey. So stay with that metaphor of that Tetris block or a game of Tetris. You're looking for that one key block that will help you open up multiple other blocks of thought opportunities, avenues in science and so on and so forth. So this word's purpose is very, very, very compelling.

You know, set up on purpose, let me oblige to my own life very early on, I discovered that my purpose in life is not just to have a good time or not just to pursue material success or anything. But as a teenager, I was thrust into a situation where I had to literally fend for not just myself, but for my family as well. And that became my driving factor in life at that age. Since the time I was 16, 17 onwards, I was catapulted into a scenario, a situation where I had to literally change the way I think, change the way I behave, change the way I make choices, and then leave a whole lot of other dysfunctional behaviors outside. The purpose today for me seems to be to just make a tangible difference in the world with my work, a tangible difference, meaning I could feel the number of lives impacted that I could see changed lives and transformed lives.

So what's your driving factor? What's your purpose? Take a moment to answer this question. What is the single biggest reason you are pursuing this leadership? book? That is the definition of purpose in companies. The purpose is to make profit for companies to make a difference in the lives of their customers. The purpose is becoming an increasingly fashionable word and we will spend more time on it. But the first element of leadership is purpose.

He/She Gets The Difference Between The Fundamental Competing

Renaissance leaders balance the need for achievement versus need for affiliation. David McClelland first came up with this grid for need for achievement versus need for affiliation, and he put it on two axes which talked about this need for achievement is your personal quest, your drive to go out and get results for your success. But the need for affiliation or the need for connection, the need for relationships is the other element that keeps you in the corporate or the business world accountable. We know of CEOs who have these outrageous fees and so on, but we also know CEOs who take significant pay cuts and let some of that be shared by their employees.

Of book, they are far and few between. But the point is there are these CEOs and these senior leaders who are not only going on their personal quest to achieve the best version of themselves and get the bottom line and top line revenues and and and get a lot of accolades and so on. But they're also taking along with them the people that have been serving them for a long time. And a good Renaissance leader, the one that you could potentially be, strives to seek a balance between personal success and success of others around in contributing to their success, you find in one of your achievements as well. But for the most part, you'll either find leaders who are moving to the one direction of just the people pleasing country club type of managers or these bad taskmasters or bad with relationships who only get the job done.

It cannot be either or if you are a Renaissance leader, if you truly want to be a Renaissance leader, you have to get both your results and your relationships right. Very early on, I learned and I decided and I watch to myself that I will never go only in the direction of results and special responsibilities. I always wanted to be known as someone who's likable, relatable, humble, a top servant leader and other top seven leaders. Might sound like a contradiction in terms, but I wanted to be seen as somebody who's willing to invest in relationships as much as in personal success. I wouldn't have come this far if I did not find that the paradigm of serving others works very well for me.

I have trained over 10000 engineers in all the years in my company for literally no material benefit. I did it because it's outside the scope of my day job. I enjoy training. I enjoyed sharing my knowledge with people. So I ended up just going and investing in people. And today, many of the folks that I taught are great ambassadors for the work I do and the values I stand. And I find myself always being called upon in situations to mediate, to counsel, to coach and to share some more of my expertise, because they actually saw me benefit from the passion and the expertise that I bring to my organization. How good are you at balancing your need for achievement versus need for affiliation, need for relationships versus the need for results? Take a moment and examine your match.

A Modern Leader Knows That He Needs To Ride High Or Lie Low

You know, a couple of years ago, I took an assignment to go to Silicon Valley and during my many trips to the beaches, I actually went and saw how surfing is a very popular sport on the West Coast. And as I studied and understood that, I thought today's world of Vuko was a volatile, uncertain, complex and ambiguous world. A sunflower is an appropriate metaphor for leadership as the leaders who are navigating this troubled time can wait in anticipation of the next wave. You're not a surfer. I do know an awful lot about the sport, but a surfer always is just prepared and is waiting to ride the next wave. And, you know, the interesting thing about just riding the wave is to actually not let the wave's energy sort of submerge them, but stay on top of that energy. And it means crouching in that position. It means just timing it perfectly.

It means that you let the energy of the wave carry you into the place where you want to go in the post pandemic world. How does that translate into meaningful action to us, you might ask? I'm glad you did. The way it works is that the really altered world offers many opportunities for us to start off immediately. Harness things have changed. So what does it mean, therefore, to the industry that you're in? Are you and your teams prepared to work in the new era and reorient yourself to see how your customers are behaving? It just changes the game completely. And instead of just living in denial about what happened, if you are already ready to ride the wave, then the future is all for you to anticipate and embrace.

Practically speaking, what are some new skills that you need, some of the skills that you need immediately are very decisive decision making, quick decision making, very fast action. Can you move into action very fast? Can you roll out products very fast? Can you. Right. And roll out your content very fast. Can you take daring steps to fall and and therefore improvise as you keep going along? The surfboard leaders are excellent metaphors for the post pandemic leaders that are bound to enter the workplace and the marketplace. Take a moment and ask yourself, am I reorienting my skills, my behavior and my mindset to embrace the post pandemic war.

The New Age Leader Is A Digital Maestro

Hey, everyone. The Renaissance leader, a leader who was in the post pandemic era, is a digital leader. What do I mean by that? If one year ago somebody asked you to do stuff on Zoome and Martiens and Vivax and any other digital channels, many common people who are not in the technology industry or who are not really digitally savvy would have rolled their eyes and said, oh, that's too much of digital media taking over our lives and so on. But the pandemic changed everything. And now families, people who've never been on the right side of digital technologies are forced to embrace the juggernaut of this technology that's enveloping us.

So the first takeaway for you and this book is if you want to be a post pandemic leader or become a leader of stature in the new economy, as we start to revive in the digital world, you have to master digital skills. You have to demonstrate leadership in the digital world. So look around you, look around all the things that you do and see how we were forced to adapt to a new reality, new situation, new new way of communication, new way of doing things. So are you in an industry which means that you have to revisit your skills and adapt to technology? You know, growing up, I had my foundational years in advertising. And the very first thing that the world of advertising got taken over by was the advent of Macintosh computers.

Macs, as we now know that back in the day, Macs were only used by these high designers and high end creative people. And if anybody was able to use a Mac, they were like the cat's whiskers. They were like this, almost like this halo effect and leaders who would walk around with an aura that was unrivaled. But today, Macintoshes are an alternative form of computing, not as operational as the Windows based computers or laptops, but Macintoshes have democratized advertising and so on. So just drawing the parallel from there today, everyone around the world, we are engulfed by the pandemic.

And what has come out as a result of that is a new world where everything is digital. Right from the way we shop, the way we commute, the way we buy things has changed everything. So a new leader, a Renaissance leader who is born through this pandemic is a digital leader. And I want to keep coming back to this theme and refrain from this late model that digital is a key component of leadership, digital leadership. What do I mean by that? It means that whether you are researching, whether you are writing, whether you are computing, whether you are just doing anything, there is a big component of your life that is digital and good leaders understand that. And if you are technology shy, you will be left behind. So a Renaissance leader is a digital leader. And I want to ask you, how are you doing in embracing these digital technologies? Are you somebody who gets excited by it or is somebody exhausted by it? Take a moment to reflect on how you're doing as a digital leader.

Leaders Are Measured For Performance

The next be in leadership is. The bottom line, word performance. You know, you get into a job based on potential, but you stay at the job based on your performance. Potential is recognized, but it's actually a performance that's regarded as a leader always, always stepping up to the plate to perform. And in the world of advertising that I come from, there's a saying that says you're only as good as your last campaign. Meaning, if your last campaign was successful, then you have a shot at the next one. Otherwise, you're only talking about Old Glory, past track record, past trophy's no one cares about. I want to remind you that great leaders take this whole notion of performance to a very, very obsessive level, because ultimately this whole set of chapters that I'm putting together, they should work.

They should in fact, they should transform lives. Otherwise, this book is a failure. Whatever you're doing online today, if it has some benefits to you, then it's those tools that you acquired or the ideas that you are acquiring, what do you benefit? Ultimately, leaders are measured by their performance. A high degree of performance orientation sets people apart when it comes to leadership skills. Back in the day when I was, you know, again in advertising, I used to think, oh, my job is to just be this. If the creators were bad, then the campaign failed. You can assign blame to others, but ultimately a leader should say the buck stops with me right here. And only those kind of very self driven performing type of leaders get to places in the business world, in the corporate world, in any sphere.

Actually, even in the world of sports, the ones who are performing all the time keep the scoreboard, picking the scoreboard reflects their performance. So what is your approach to performance orientation? Do you thrive in this race against the clock or does it put pressure on you? Do you enjoy looking at the scoreboard value performing or do you just give it your best on the field and then worry about the scoreboard later, no matter what your orientation is? If you have performance on the top of your mind, then you're able to say you're a very successful leader, a successful leader counts and makes everything count. His ability to count and make everything else count brings his leadership to the top.

If this one element in this ever seven piece, it is very important that people look to plans, people look to priorities, but ultimately they also benchmark you, major you against the performance that you've delivered within a particular quarter, a particular time capsule within a year, no matter what your tenure inside of an organization is, what matters is how you performed.

The New Age Leader Starts With Seeing The Invisible

You cannot live past your vision. What do I mean by that, a leader's capacity to live? The influence to produce results is in direct relation to the vision a person has for his or her life. Think about it, think about all your journey so far, whether it's college or whether it's early days at work or already in your work experience, entrepreneurial journey, the larger your vision and your capability to dream and have a plan for your life, you are likely to achieve it. So in this chapter, I want to explore this whole notion of what does a Renaissance leader have for his vision? What does it mean to have a vision for your life? And a very pivotal question, because while you're keen to develop your leadership in this World Vision has actual implications for every aspect of your life. It will affect your relationships.

It'll affect your finances. It will affect your ability for you to go out and spend your time in exchange for whatever you're aspiring for. In short, everything you do is a function of your vision. So let me ask you, what is your vision? And here I'm not talking about just having the vision boards for your life where you are setting goals. Yes, the goal setting is an important part of your vision, boarding and setting a future that you would like to have. But what really is your vision for yourself and the world around you? I want you to start grappling with this, because if there's any element that determines whether you will be a successful leader or not, it is your vision. And sometimes vision.

Evolving at different stages in your life, you just keep having different visions to guide your life by it, but at the stage you are right now, what is the vision for your life? How would you spend the rest of your life? Because that's where you're going. And vision is always linked to the future. It doesn't mean that I'm currently thinking about what to do for pleasure or something today. It doesn't mean that it is always into the future. It's distant. It impacts your plans for the future. Ever since I was a child, I must tell you, ever since I was a child, I was almost intuitively drawn to this whole world of vision and. I, I, I wish I could tell you that I chanced upon my vision for life as early as when I was a child or when I was in my younger years.

No, I staggered my way around like most young people and just did not know where I was going. But once I had that vision and I had this epiphany type of meeting where I changed my perspective towards my life. Everything, as they say, was history. My priorities changed, my relationships changed, my ability to manage finances, my ability to make good use of my time changed simply in the light of my vision. So in simple terms, let me define what a vision is, a vision is a simple blueprint that you have for your life. A simple blueprint that encompasses your people. It encompasses your family, it encompasses your time. It encompasses your finances. It encompasses everything you do sort of goes through a blues blueprint.

And that's how you live. And the larger the blueprint, the larger the vision, the more impactful and influential your life will be. So what are you planning to make out of your life? You know, one of the inspirational questions actually that I heard in a book by Stephen Covey is what would you do with your wild and precious one single life? What would you do with your one single wild and precious life? Makes you think it's very inspirational. If you know, you can dream big dreams, there's a Jewish proverb that says young people shall see great visions and why young people? Because young people are considered to be these ambitious, brash, risk averse. Dynamic, bold, audacious thinkers, right? So what is the most audacious goal and vision you can think of? If you were to if everything you plan from here on were to become real, what is the grandest vision you can think of? Just do not think of real realistic terms, do not think of barriers and self limiting beliefs directing all the things that could go wrong.

Forget it for a moment. Think if everything goes right, if everything you are assuming and dreaming would go right, how would that vision look like? Take a moment, think in color, think in vivid, clear specifics, let your imagination draw, because the Vorster, the vision you have, the more likely you will set yourself to live that ambitious, more dynamic life. I can't challenge you enough because the vision that I have for my future and for my family, my influence on this world is huge and I hope it'll be as big. So take a moment and. Involve yourself in this free flowing exercise and ask yourself if everything is a dream come true, what would my vision look like for the future? Take a moment, take some time and spend time on that exercise.

The New Age Leader Has A Vision With A Deep Core And Broad

So we agreed that vision has one element of just blueprint in your plan. The view of the world. But now I want to just take it one level lower and talk to you about the two elements that constitute this whole region casting. When you cast a vision for the world around you and for your life specifically. There are two parts to it. One is this whole notion of capacity. Now, what do I mean by capacity? It means the sum total of all of your dreams. It means the sum total of your skills. It means the sum total of your willingness. It means the sum total of your aspirations and the price you're willing to pay in pursuit of that vision.

If my vision is to become this worldchanging communicator, as is my vision, by the way. I need to be able to outline that vision in very vivid terms as to what those exact aspirations mean. By way of beating the scores, I am in the park fulfilling a sliver of that aspiration to change the world through my communication skills. That's my vision. Likewise, I encourage you to start thinking, if you are having an idea of a product or if you are wanting to grow in the corporate or business world, or if you want to change the world, go into teaching, go into some sector which involves actual real life transformation and the people around you, by all means, you should commit yourself to that capacity building. Your capacity should be in direct proportion to the size of your vision.

If you have a small vision, then you don't need an awful lot of capacity, but if you have this huge vision that that gives you goosebumps, that gives you chills, that gives you adrenaline rush, then you also need to have those kind of capacities that will just make you sit up and in the middle of the night with excitement. You know, I always dreamt of living an inspirational life, and to some degree, I think I was able to achieve that dream. But when this vision crêpes you. It's your capacity that starts changing, either you let the capacity build your vision or you let the vision build your capacity. In my case, I had this vision first and I set about increasing my capacity to go out and achieve that. In other words, people call it bandwidth, in other words, people call it.

The energy you bring to in pursuit of your dreams, you know, in sports parlance, we talk about shining stars and burn out leaders are a spent force. Right. The phrase spent force comes to mind. Your vision. Is action capacity actually directly linked to that term or are you going to be a shining star or a spent force in pursuit of that vision? If you fall short of your vision and you're not achieved it, then which means you kind of fell short. But if you end up achieving that vision, you're called a shining star. And therein is the ability for you to navigate how much energy you bring to the other capacity you bring in fulfilling that vision. The deeper your capacity, the larger your capacity, the higher the chances of you achieving your vision, otherwise you'll be a burnout, you'll be a spent force and the ability for you to. But 100 percent of your effort is a function of how exciting that vision is.

You know, great entrepreneurs, people would change the world. You look at Tesla, you look at Apple, you look at Google, you look at any product that is changing the world. And the core of it or behind it are people who have this audacious vision for the world to be different by virtue of their contribution. What is your vision looking like? Do you have the capacity to go after your vision? Full force is unstoppable, relentless. In a manner that just makes you go. Successful. Take a moment and ask yourself in relation to my vision, how is my capacity? In relation to my vision, how is my capacity? Am I willing to go and I want to explore the whole notion of commitment in the separate chapter, but in relation to your vision, how large is your capacity?

This Leader Lives By The Rule Book Definition

If you ask me what? Mr. Robert, is your definition of leadership or this New Age leadership? I would just say almost simplistically, the definition is someone who can inspire people and drive results is a new HBO inspired. People drive results. If you can do those two elements, you are a leader in my book. Inspire people, drive results, you can memorize this till it becomes a part of the top of your mind, recall an inspirational leader who is willing to deliver results. That's all there leadership if you do a Google search on the topic of leadership. There are more than ten thousand books available.

And all of them come at it from various perspectives, various slants, various principles, paradigms, but in my view, if there's something as simple as somebody who can galvanize people around me and get to a desired state of results. Leadership definition is that we tend to complex five things more than they already are. In my view, if I'm able to be liked by others, just get people to like me and they do things for me. I'm already influencing them. And I, I fulfill that definition of being a leader. Now, I may not be on the cover of a Forbes magazine or a Fortune magazine or on the CNBC channel. None of those are industry leaders and industry captains and heads of large corporations.

To me, that's my definition of leadership. Those are titles. Those are rules that they got to adopt as a result of a series of years of experiences and achievements. But for our purposes, the definition is whether you are at home or whether you're in a small team, whether you're a small business that you're working for the three people organization, or your ability to inspire people around you and get stuff done is leadership, in my view. So where do you stand in this definition? Take a moment to reflect upon it and then we'll continue this conversation.

The Leader's Currency Is Influence - Moving People Through Example

I want to introduce you to the currency or the calling card or the operating principle of a new age leader and what is the influence? You know, New Age leaders, the Renaissance leaders don't use their titles or their track record or their pedigree for moving ahead in life, they use influence. What do I mean by that? They know that in the world of business or in the world of corporate equations, change quickly. And so what you hold as a title cannot be your calling card, your calling card ought to be the influence that you have inside the organization. What do I mean by influence? What's the definition of influence that influences what people think of you when you're not in the room? Influence is what people are willing to do for you, even when you are not in the room, on the phone, on the phone or in the meeting.

Influence is this invisible currency that you are able to carry and use it and convert it into real time action activity when you need to. So in other words, influence is like a series of deposits that you make into your own leadership bank account. Just like we have money fighting up in our bank account, influence is the currency that you build into your capital, into your bank as your journey along the leadership path. The greater your influence, the greater your ability to convert it and get things done for you or your team or for your people. The less of the influence, the more you're asking for people to do favors for you. Now, even when you ask people for a favor, what's the phrase you use? Thanks for doing this. I owe you one.

And so even when in a situation you call people to do favors for you, you're always. Using some of that currency that you built as influence in exchange for the favors, you know, one of my most heartening moments was when I moved from my hometown to a big city in India for a new job. And. As is my demeanor, I would just stop at every workstation and say hi to colleagues and build conversations, and since I was new, I didn't have any known friends inside the organization. But what stood me in good stead was my personality, some of the skills that I had learned by then to kind of go and build my relationships ground up and over a period of time, I really became close to most people in the organization.

I've had my share of detractors. I've had my share of people who robbed me the wrong way. Potentially, I would have robbed them the wrong way. God knows what happened. But I did have people who did not really wear my speed dial with our friends. The friendships that I built with the not so important people in the organization really stood me in good stead, for example. How often do you make friends with, let's say, the gatekeepers and the organizations, the people who are not seen as the C-level leaders or the movers and shakers in the organizations, people who are in the administrative staff, people who are not in the glamorous roles, your ability to build relationships with them is as crucial if you want to be a leader of influence.

So I built some of these friendships. And soon the time came for me to leave that organization. Some of the tributes, some of the feedback that I got was so inspiring. In fact, one colleague who was instrumental and she was working with her boss and even at the stage of me being considered for that post, shared with me how many people actually competed for that role. And I got to know about that only because of the fact that I was able to build this trust based relationship with this colleague and she said, you really came with a lot of pedigree and a track record because some of the people we had interviewed had even sort of outsized qualifications in the in the in the in terms of the business schools that they came from, graduated from.

I would have never known that fact if it were not for the fact that I built that friendship with some of those colleagues and they shared their insight, insights about me before I joined that organization. I hope that gives you an example of what influence can do for you. Influence is this combined capital that you build inside an organization or in your network that you can call out in exchange for your goals, in achievement of your goals, in pursuit of your vision.

A Leader Keeps Providing The Resources To Make Everyone Successful

One piece that defines a leadership role is one of provision. You know, as a leader, sometimes they acquire almost like a maternal figure or a paternal figure, depending on the type of personality you bring to the table. A leader is always seen as someone who is not just a taskmaster, who gets done, but also somebody who nurses and nurtures and delicately panders to the people on the team. In one of my favorite definitions of leadership is a leader is a dispenser of hope. And I love that way it is phrased. It's a dispenser of hope, just that vision of a leader providing an unending supply of hope just fills my heart with joy, because hope is one important element that drives everyone's collective future.

You look at this chapter with the hope that it will make a difference. You're taking this book in the hope that it will transform your life. You're hoping that some of the skills that you are acquiring will give you an edge in the marketplace. You get a dream job or you start up and you do something as an entrepreneur, no matter what you do. It's that fundamental belief and a hope that your life will be better because of some of the things we are doing. And a leader's job becomes a provider of hope, a provider of resources, a provider of morale, a provider of a sense of well-being that that word of encouragement, in fact, the word encouragement has built into it courage.

So when things are not doing well or when somebody in the team is not doing well, it is that leader who comes along and provides that hopeful courage that things will get better, that he or she can fix it. Now, I don't mean all of these mushy, soft, happy things all the time. Touchy feely thing about leaders, there are times when you have to crack the whip. There are times when you have to get them to reorient and focus on the big goal and the performance elements. Dixon. So I do want to make sure that I'm not moving to the other extreme, but the provision role of a leader determines how well he provides for his own team. Does he fight for his team? Does he protect his team? You know, the image of a shepherd comes to my mind.

I grew up in Asia. I grew up in India, and a shipload always carries a shepherd's staff on a stick and that stick is just. A symbol that the ship not only is under the strength of the leader, but the shepherd protects the sheep on his people from external attacks, that stick will really protect any other wild animal from attacking the sheep. So that's a powerful metaphor for me to just leave this segment on the seven pieces of leadership where a leader is a dispenser of hope. What sort of a leader do you want to be? Do you want to be a leader who just thrives on open builds and instills hope around you? Or do you want to be a leader who just is focused on performance? Take a moment to reflect on your leadership style.

There Is Always A Way Because This Leader Is Dynamic

Here's an exciting topic that might energize you. You know, very early in my life, I had this vision of being a dynamic leader. The word dynamic comes from the Latin word dunamis which is the same word that gave us the English word dynamo, which is a power house, a generator of energy. If I were to ask you, are you a dynamo of energy? Chances are you'd say, well, my personality doesn't lend itself to be a dynamo of energy, I'm an introvert. I don't know, sometimes I could be dynamic, sometimes I cannot, no matter what your personality makeup is. You have to have dynamism as you pursue your vision. Let me just give you a few, a few more.

I love letters that work together and I love letters that form an acronym. I love letters because it makes communication easier and it sticks with the audience. So let me ask you, do you know the 3G of living your vision, the 3G where you have goals related to your vision? And you have the gusto that is needed to go, that the gusto is the energy and the power and the dynamism that is needed to get you goals and the gusto that you need. And the third element is the gifts that you need to use, the strength that you need to use in pursuit of your goals. Let me bring them all together. Let's say I want to. Become rich.

That's not a real goal, it's a dream, let's say I want to become a millionaire by the time in the next, let's say, five years. Now you are saying this is my goal. And how I go about it is a function of my Gustl, my energy, my willingness to pay the price towards that goal. But what I need to do in pursuit of that goal is really the gifts and the strength that I need to deploy in pursuit of that goal. So goals are the end result that you want to achieve. Gifts are what you need to do or what friends that you need to deploy. And gusto is how fast you can get? What is the velocity with which you go?

On one side, I want you to write your goals and on the other side, write your gifts. And in the middle of town called Gustl, how fast are you willing to go or how much of a capacity are you willing to bring to get your gifts deployed in pursuit of your goals? If you want. And the last can be the gold at the end of the rainbow. The pot of gold that you're pursuing at the end of the rainbow. It could be a proverb, it could be metaphorical. But you understand what I'm saying. It's the end result. What you see as the final outcome of what you want to achieve is a function of your custom. I really want to encourage you and say right from my younger years as I set out to be the dynamic leader.

Things started coming together. You start rallying people behind you who are willing to help you. Doors open, sometimes doors get closed. But if you're dynamic, you keep knocking doors over and over again and then doors finally open. And you do come to the end of the rainbow. I want to challenge you if you want to be a dynamic leader, the new age dynamic leader will ask you, how is your costume on a scale of one to 10? Where would you place yourself in terms of your costume level?

It's Never About Time Management, Always About Priorities

Show your friends and I will tell you who you are. My dad and my mom used to just keep on repeating that I used to roll my eyes and I would just say, oh, come on, you. Some of these phrases that you hear in childhood actually determine your destiny, actually determine where you go, and there is a lot of wisdom in some of these scenes that you hear. Show me your friends and I will tell you who you are. Taking that analogy forward, I would like to ask you to show me your calendar and I can tell you who you are. Show me your calendar and I can tell you who you are. What do I mean by that? You know, between. In this pandemic between your one desk and your bed and your screen.

Your days are disappearing, right? This seems like a Bermuda Triangle between your bed, your work and maybe a TV or a screen. How often do you realize that this is just gone by in a blur and you're not even sure what you've accomplished? Those days are days when. You've either really done something productive or you just binge watched something or you are just allowing a lot of content to come your way and you have no idea how your day went. So if you are like me who struggles to keep up with all the distractions that come at you, this is one principle that you want to remember. Your calendar is guided by your vision. We explored how our vision is going to be the blueprint by which one we can live as a leader.

But here I want to build further and see if your calendar is not capturing elements of your vision, then you're just wasting time. Early, you might say, oh, no, I'm in a job which does not allow me to capture my parts of the vision, then I'm afraid then you have to make some adjustments to your calendar and to do the vision that you have. You cannot be going in the direction of your dreams and letting your calendar just be controlled by outside forces. So the first principle I want to teach is that you have to own your calendar and guard zealously. You cannot let outside. Forces just come and knock you over and upset your calendar. In the advertising world, where I come from is to be a saying that said, your lack of planning should not become an emergency on my part.

Your lack of planning should not become an emergency on my part, and if you worked in the corporate world or if you're an entrepreneur, you know that sometimes what you're planning for your day is not exactly the way it will pan out. And I understand that. But for the most part, if you are in control of your calendar, then you still have some time left to manage these unexpected emergencies that tend to topple you over and all of them important, all of them urgent. Then by the time you finish all the agencies and all the emergencies, then you'll have precious little time to worry about your calendar. So we explored a vision, but your vision has to be tied to your calendar. A leader, a Renaissance leader, a leader in the New Age has a mastery of his calendar in extension, his time.

How good are you at protecting your kind ? How good are you at first of all, planning your calendar? And how good are you at thinking in terms of hours? You know, you always think of one little episode. Right, one little phone call or one, and before you know it, that call has just dragged into a half hour or 20 minutes and hour on that little episode has now become two, three episodes. And lo and behold, I'm not against watching for entertainment, but that needs to be as planned as well. I, for one, use such entertainment channels as rewards to the work I've already put in. So I sort of on my end, it was just like I binge on some foods only after a run, so I want to challenge you to start thinking about how to start planning for your calendar and how to protect your calendar as you advance in the life of your vision. Great leaders not only live by a vision, but they also have a mastery of their time. Great leaders have a mastery of their time.

This Guide Has An Unflappable Temperament In The Face Of Difficulties

Renaissance leaders have a strong internal locus of control, you know, when I first learned it in my MBA school, this whole notion of locus of control, I felt as if this concept of locus of control, which is by the definition, means that a leader has a strong sintering, a strong grounding about himself. So the locus of control means that he is centered, anchored, grounded in his own personality, and he will not let external factors shake him or sway him or disturb him, unless, of book, something like shattering critical happens. Right. In that sense, he is not easily disruptive, but he is not easily distractible. And that lends itself to make him invincible almost to a certain degree. So how do you develop this locus of control? I'm glad you asked me.

Renaissance leaders committed because of their internal compass, their internal navigating system, their internal values system, the guiding principles that we talked of so often. Their whole approach to failure and success is almost like equal treatment with equanimity, as that famous Rudyard Kipling poem suggests, says they look at both success and failure as impostors to be not trusted. But that doesn't mean that they are not driven. That doesn't mean they're not performers. That doesn't mean that they don't give everything in the battlefield, nor that it doesn't mean that what it means is why they are so focused on the inputs and the process of winning.

They will not let the outcomes determine how they respond to it. And the same is true of the way they handle bad news inside a team, the way they handle anything that is not so positive that is going on in the lives of a team, a customer escalation or some kind of unpleasant situation. They are routed because they have a strong sense of this locus of control. Another element of this strong locus of control, in addition to their centering, in addition to the compass, is the clarity with which they drive towards their destination. Again, they have a longish view of their goal and vision. May they know how to take the short term bumps along the way.

And so that clarity lends them to really accept any short term setbacks or defeats on the way. You know, it's always great to work with leaders who have that almost detached almost kamik almost, you know, unattached sort of mindset to day to day operations. Those leaders are a delight to work with, but there are those other leaders who have a very weak center of focus, locus of control, and then they are easily swayed by something. I mean, you're scared to tell them any bad news. You're scared to deliver anything that is not something that they want to hear. And as a result, what happens is all the followers and surrounding team members only tell them stuff that they'd like to hear.

Which sort of defeats the whole trust element, because they are not prepared for any unpleasant or disturbing news and do their best to only play to the gallery or make them hear what they'd like to hear. And so a leader is developing a big blind spot right there. Renaissance leaders, on the other hand, know that nothing can really sway them or shape them. And they keep moving on in the pursuit of the next goal. And the next day, that intuitive sense of timing allows them to have a longer view of the projects that they are working and therefore it contributes to their strong sense of their locus of control.

Locusts means stand locusts means anchoring locusts means that how is your locus of control? Are you a person who falls apart when things don't go wrong? Right. Or are you OK to sort of build things, scenarios that allow you to deal with life in a cool, calm, composed manner when things don't go right? Take a moment to reflect on this element of locus of control.

It Is Always The Right Time To Do The Right Thing!

Renaissance leaders have an excellent sense of timing. And you might wonder, what does the word timing mean here, you know how when you tell yourself things to do in the future, when you have a vision to accomplish, you're always waiting for a better time to do things. Well, it turns out that there is never going to be a time where things will be better. And life always rewards those who sort of get into action, get the momentum behind them and keep moving to make progress rather than waiting for the right perfect time to come and see the high seas. Imagine if you are a sailor, imagine if you are somebody who is a risk taker, you're waiting for the conditions. Where the risk is of a failure is literally zero.

And only then you would try something that would be ludicrous, wouldn't it? Ben is a seasoned sailor or a seasoned runner or a seasoned person just decides that no matter what the circumstances are, you would always just get out of the door and then start waiting to navigate the difficulties around the whole journey and your ship and your boat and so on. So using that sailboat metaphor, using the fact that you are on the seas, there will never be a time when it is perfectly conducive. The sea is calm and the water is tranquil. And then you are able to make us smooth sailing along along your path that you set out for yourself.

There will never be a great timing that is ideal for your sailing. Take that into your life and ask yourself this question. What are the things that I'm postponing or keeping just in abeyance, waiting for the perfect time, the right time? There is no such thing as the right time. If it is in your vision, if it is compelling you to do something, you have to take massive action. You have to take baby steps, even if they have to be. But just keep moving one day at a time, one step at a time. You know, I have a teenage son and I just kind of coached him and made him do a half marathon the very first time. He was one of the first boys in this age group on Friends Circle to do a half marathon.

And then young friends get together and they say, Hey, buddy, how did you do it? In a very understated way. He said, Yeah, I don't know, man. I just kept putting one foot in front of the other. And I thought that was a very powerful metaphor for me as a dad and as a leadership coach to take and say that's a great, great metaphor to capture this notion of how to take action just one step at a time, putting one foot out the other. And then this young lad was able to just finish a half marathon along with me. Likewise, Renaissance leaders never wait for a better time or a time or a perfect time to get into action. They just put one foot in front of the other and then just keep moving.

What are some of the goals you set for yourself this year? And why are they still in your Excel sheet or in your vision board or on your whatever, you captured them? What action are you taking in terms of moving forward with these? If you are not taking action, there will still be a passive written mode unless you take action. So realisms leaders have come to be known as those who do not wait for the right time. They just keep moving one step at a time, taking action.

For A Truly Committed Leader The Spoils Come After A Labor Of Love!

One of the mantras that I live by is a phrase called ground always precedes glory. Grain always precedes glory. What do I mean by that? And it's actually an inspiration that I got, by the way, I phrase that line and it came as a natural outcome of my marathon pursuits and my running pursuits. But what do I mean by grind? Always preceding the glory. You know, we often. Want to become leaders or you always want a certain thing because of the perceived glamor that is associated with it. Very often, if you see the cost of the price you need to pay to get to that glamor, the grain that is involved, maybe you may not pursue that. We always judge people by the glorious side, but the glamorous side.

But we never often see how the sausage is being made, so to speak. The amount of time these elite athletes, business leaders, the amount of time they spend honing their craft, honing their skills, if you see it is just mind boggling, the effort, the sweat, the single minded discipline and dedication that they have to their craft. It's just unbelievable the amount of effort that goes into in pursuit of that glamor. Renaissance leaders understand it. Renaissance leaders know that without the grind, without the cross, there is no crown. Leadership is almost always likened to a cross like a king always wears a cross.

They see the crown, but they don't often see the cross or the price that they pay to be a leader. Think about all the leaders in your own circle, your family, your extended family, your work, your business leaders, your role models, entrepreneurs, you never see them just indulge in mindless chatter are aimless activities. They always are very purpose driven because by definition, leadership clones go to those who have actually carried the leadership cross. So while these metaphors are all great for you. What I want you to really grapple with is this is a very unpopular concept. In some instant gratification generation, your field leaders are just popped like microwave popcorn and then inside of my microwave, it doesn't work like that.

It takes years of varnishing one's skills, years of practicing and fine tuning, their communication, their goal setting, their ability to navigate and facilitate things and work together in collaborative manners in order to dedicate their life to a life of success. So do you get attracted to Renaissance leadership because of the crown, because of the glamor or because of the perceived success that goes with it? Then I want to challenge you, you need to be prepared to carry the cross that goes along with the background, that goes along with the willingness to put your head down when when others are not working, the willingness to do an unthinkable stuff in the way it calls for sacrifices of your time, effort when when it is just way too easy to turn on the TV and children. So are you prepared to make the sacrifices that are necessary to get to the crown? That's the challenge I wanted to place before you.

This New Era Calls For New Paradigms - This One Is For You

One of the fundamental paradigms that Renaissance leaders live by is about the people around them, do they see them as problems to be fixed or do they see them as potential? Holders that need just rekindling that need a spark if it is a problem orientation, you come at it as a no at all. I'm going to fix you guys' kind of mindset, but with potential. Carriers are carriers of potential mines. It allows them to just spot the right conversations and drive them to better performance. Another element that drives them is a fundamental belief that every situation or every person has the ability to transform or change, given the right motivations and the right incentives. You know, have you heard the term that so-and-so is a gone case in India? I used to hear that phrase a lot. So-and-so is a gone case or a lost case.

That's so bad, you cannot write off somebody as a lost case or a gun case just because you've had repeated failures or perceived repeated resistance from them to change. Who are you to say that they are a lost case or a gun case? Everyone has potential and the willingness provided it's like a combination lock. I wish there was a simpler analogy, but I think the key to human motivation is like a combination. It's a combination of three or four factors that need to come together. The ability for the person to be Howard felt validated, open enough so that they can hear the right words of advice and with the right words of advice, fall into that person. Some magic happens and a light bulb goes on.

Leaders always invariably take this almost maternal sort of an approach to team members around them, saying every individual has the potential to change, given enough incentives and motivation. Now, that's where the Vietnam question comes in. What's in it for me if you answer that? Sometimes that combination might open. If you sometimes answer that, your potential, I see potential in you to open up a lot more avenues. Back in the day when I was struggling as a young leader, when somebody talked to me about potential, it just lifted a burden off my shoulders and set me up for future growth and possibilities. Nobody gave me a shot and somebody came along and said, I see potential in you. And those words of encouragement set me up forever, almost on the on the verge of committing suicide.

I turned my story around and mine is a very powerful redemption story. I believe with all my heart, it works when you look into somebody and say, I see potential, I see potential for greatness, then you are the Nasdaq's leader. Renaissance leaders carry this powerful image that people are carriers of potential, limitless potential, boundless potential. And all it takes is the right word, the right spark to get them going. Take a moment to ask yourself, did anyone speak to you in those encouraging terms? If so, what does it take for you to realize your own potential? Renaissance leaders are constantly driving people to live up to their potential to realize their potential.

Another Paradigm Shift For This Leader....

Here's another wonderful tool that Verizon's leaders embrace. You know, talk of climbing the corporate ladder, climbing the corporate ladder, climbing, going to the top of the pyramid. Renaissance leaders replace the word ladder with Roller-Coaster. Have you ever seen the lines or how people wait in anticipation outside the entrance of a roller coaster? I don't know if you are an adrenaline junkie like me, but I'm an adrenaline junkie and much to the dismay of all my family members, I, along with my eight year old, are pretty much the only ones who are dying to go on a roller coaster. My life and the other side, they're scared of some of these and they don't ever come on them. But why? Why do people wait for hours in these theme parks or these amusement parks to go on a roller coaster that lasts maybe a minute or a couple of minutes at best? Think about it.

The amount of time taken outside and the waiting area is a fraction of the adventure itself is just a fraction of the amount of time taken while you wait outside. But the wait is worth it because of the sheer exhilaration and the euphoria and the thrill of what happens on that adventure. Think of your leadership journey as an adventure and life becomes suddenly a thrilling experience. You wait during your non exciting moments as if you're waiting at the roller coaster, when the big moment comes, you ride it, you ride the rollercoaster, and then you're back on the ground waiting for the next instant. If you think of it like an ascent, you're thinking like a mountain climber or a huge rock climber. You're already succeeding. And no wonder they call it lonely at the top.

He doesn't have to be like that. Have you ever seen a rollercoaster of one person going and just having all the fun by himself? Usually people go with their families and friends, right? And so when I call leadership a team sport, that's what it becomes. You're taking your whole team on an adventure. You work with your team, you're having this drive these crazy projects that you do on crazy deadlines. The adrenaline is shared among the team because you are thinking adventure and not necessarily ascent and how this project might help you get to the next level. Don't always think Essent think adventure. How might this shift from ascent to adventure help you in your own career journey? Take a moment to reflect on that and see if you need to reorient your thinking from ascent to adventure and keep moving along in your career trajectory.

A Critical Aspect Of These Leaders Is They Don't Fit The Mold

Renaissance leaders are mavericks. What do I mean by that? America is someone who comes into a place where conventional rules are being followed and he just decides to defy or rewrite his or their rules. And the same is true of a Renaissance leader. Everything you knew about leadership has now changed. The rules of old school do not apply anymore, which means you've got to make your own rules as you fly and you keep going along. And so if you are a leader of any core material strength, you need to actually start writing your own rules. And there are many people who pay lip service to those who keep failing and stuff. But you need to be a maverick.

You need to embody this whole notion of breaking rules. You know, just recently, I was the CMO of a startup in the Silicon Valley, and in my time there, I was willing to push the rules and rewrite the rules and say, hey, Tim, I'll back you up if I need to. If somebody comes to you and raps you on the knuckles, I'll be there to protect you. But let's break the rules. And I saw one time the young ones were like, oh, what do you want to break the rules? I said, you know. Let's push how far we can push and the ability for a team to know that you're willing to take risks for them, set them up for failure, and then set them up to try different things, be free spirited and try out new, exciting adventures of leadership.

What happens is because people are scared of being the embarrassment that comes when you fail at something. People are afraid of peer pressure. People are afraid that they'll lose the competitive advantage if something spectacular fails. People are always playing safe. People are playing by rules that have been proven before. And therefore, mavericks don't don't find that very challenging. They're willing to take a new approach. They're willing to try something new out. And to that degree, leaders, Renaissance leaders of the New Age break rules and make their own rules. I mean, I paid the price for being a rule breaker a couple of times in my own career, but for the most part because I did not fit into a particular mold or a role, I was constantly pushing the boundaries of my own leadership journey.

If they expected me to do certain things in order to get ahead, I wouldn't do it because I wanted to play my own way, like that famous Frank Sinatra thing. I did it my way, right. It's the ability for him to say I run this race. I ran it my way. I played the game. I played it my way. Is that remarkable legacy to leave on a team or even on yourself? Let me ask you, how comfortable are you first mastering the rules and then breaking the rules? Verizon's leaders are OK, breaking and making their own rules.

They Know The Why Aspect Of Their Compulsive Obsession To Win

One of the topics I visit in my book is why do you want to win? I want to ask you this question, why do you want to become a Renaissance leader and win at the marketplace, win at the workplace, win at being an entrepreneur, is it to make outrageous wealth? Is it to be unrivaled? Success unrivaled? No matter what your ambition and lofty goals are, the reason you want to do that is a very important aspect and usually it comes from one or two motivations. The one motivation is this ever obsessive, almost destructive need to win at everything. Their desire to make a good impression all the time, the desire to just just be out outperform everybody all the time.

Now, I don't think I am sort of discouraging excellence. I'm not for a moment disparaging excellence. I'm not even disparaging this relentless quest to improve the things around us by inventing new stuff, by solving big problems around us. No, but the point I am asking is the motivation should not come from just being this over competitive almost when at every cost sort of motivation, the corporate world is full of people who just want to win at any cost. And that's why some of their own strengths become their weaknesses.

And then hubris sets in and distrust and mistrust sets them and people around them start beginning to suffer because of that leader. Before that becomes a blind spot, I want to ask you, what is your driving motivation for winning now? Personally,

I answered that question many, many years ago. I also want to win, but I want to win not because I want to beat somebody or prove to somebody that I am better, but I want to do justice to the gifts and talents and skills and strengths that God gave me. That is my motivation. And because they come at it from a custodian mindset, I'm not exactly captive to the competitor mindset, and this is where I really want to draw the line between being a custodian of your gifts versus just out and out ruthless competitor. There's a difference.

The ruthless competitor doesn't trust anyone in his inner circle because he never, he feels threatened, could come from anywhere. In fact, threats might come from someone who is closest to him. And as a result, one is always watchful. And if you are always watching your back, you can't really live without a forward looking mindset. I want to challenge you today. What is your motivation? Is it a custodian mindset where you are looking at gifts, talents, strengths that you want to deploy because it makes you feel good and there is an adrenaline rush? That is the joy of competing. There is this joy of winning. That's great. But it is if you take it as if it's a life or death battle that you have to win at any cost.

When you lose, it just drags you down. You feel depressed. Then maybe you crossed the line between being competitive and over competitive. Take a moment today and answer this question on the spectrum of one to 10, anything between five and 10 being over competitive, are you in the over competitive range of this? And then it has a lot of dysfunctional outcomes as a result of your compulsive desire to win. Take a moment to reflect on it and see if you need to recalibrate your winning orientation.

A Leader Is A Communicator - With A Megaphone

A very important draw that every leader has to play is one of a good communicator. I have a separate chapter coming up on communication, but one cannot overstate the importance of communication in this day and age of splintered attention spans and proliferation of screens where people are just divided completely between multiple screens at work and at home and. The attention level of people to pay attention to what you have to say is significantly hampered. And this is where the great leaders' communication skills come in handy. If you want to be a leader of influence, everyone in your team needs to be on the same page and obviously you understand that metaphor of being on the same page.

It actually comes from the music world where people are reading music from the same music sheet or something, where different instruments and the rhythm chapter and the wind chapter or the keys or the strings, they're all performing to be on the same page. If you're not a leader and you have multiple people reporting to you, you need to be able to write that communication or verbally communicate in a manner that everybody is totally to you. But some leaders also play this communication game in a very different way by selective communication, they disclose some communication to some people and they don't disclose some to some. And then there's confusion. And then there is a lot of great wine. That is a lot of informal chatter that goes on in a team that sits up for a lot of dysfunctional outcomes.

A smart corporate leader or a smart business leader ensures that he is a superb communicator, communicating with clarity, communicating with timing, communicating with efficiency. Why is it important? Because if you are not constantly offering guidance and providing the necessary support to the team, the team just does their own thing and the overall effectiveness level of the team really begins to suffer. So here, the impact of a communicator really shines through when everyone on the team can see that they understand the team's motivation, the team's strategy, the team's big goal, the team's top three or four imperatives for the year are very well understood by the team.

And a leader can be all strategy that you want them all carrying, that he can be won if he's not communicating well and ensuring that the team is on the same page, marching towards the goal, the effectiveness of the overall team and to suffer. How do you rate yourself as a communicator? Do you think the emails that you write are effective enough, do you think your phone conversations are Tsoukalas or these virtual meetings? How effective are you? Take a moment to gather feedback. Do you get asked a lot of follow up questions when you say something, because if you say something and there are too many follow up questions, which means you did not communicate what you wanted to do in the first place, succinctly and clearly. So a whole lot of dynamics go into communications, which I'll be covering, but just to suffice in this chapter, the role of a communicator can never be overemphasized as a leader.

Build, Build And Build Is The Mantra For Value Creation

Another role, and this is something that you may or may not truly cherish, is the role of a builder. You know, every team leader or every leader on the fast track is a leader on an accelerated path, is out there trying to build something now. The very notion of building might presuppose that it takes an awful lot of time and some people are impatient. They want to just do this, you know, like they do it in the movies. They come in and just do this Fast and Furious type of a fight and then vanquish the enemy. But in reality, the corporate world or business world seldom operates like that. They are looking for leaders who are problem solvers, who are seasoned, who have sustained their leadership journey over a period of time and deliver results in different settings and different contexts.

So in that context, do you want to be seen as a bit of so what does it entail? What is a builder's role in a business role entails somebody who's not just driving for results, but is also taking along with him a bunch of leaders that he's building as his next level bench, next level level two leaders. You know, back in the advertising industry where I used to, I started my early days. If a particular high-Profile senior leader left. You could be pretty sure that the whole creative team left, this would be an exodus in that agency because that man would go and build his team in the new agency. And creative fields, which have high turnover or leadership industries which have high turnover, have that kind of phenomena where teams migrate like birds and migrate during winter.

Whether you are building your own team out of a vanity factor or whether you have this charismatic leader who just draws people and they like to stay with you no matter what the style that draws people to you, if you are able to look around and see people. With Underwood, with total, undiluted attention to you, then you are in a strong position as a builder. Very rarely we have a great combination of people and result oriented leaders coming together. And that's what makes this book an all too important case. I'm making a case where results don't have to be at the expense of people and people. Management doesn't have to be at the expense of sacrificing results.

A great Renaissance leader is also a builder of both performance track records as well as people. Take a moment to ask yourself, how good am I in this role of building people of sustained performance, of being able to build a product or build a service or a track record on which I can be proud of. And a whole lot of people can be proud of these two acts as a people and performance. How good are you in building a team as you keep going along? Take a moment to reflect on this role often as a leader.

Multi-Pronged Strategy Is His Middle Name. Always Planning To Make

There are many roles that a leader has to play on any given day in office. But one of the more dominant roles that they play includes one is called a strategy maker. Every day as he opens or he opens her e-mail box. Half hour, more than a big significant chunk of their effort goes into strategy making, just like, you know, in a game, a competitive game of chess or in a competitive game of where there is a lot of thinking involved, these leaders are constantly deploying their resources, their their finances, their teams bandwidth to achieve a certain end goal. So this strategy maker's hand is something that every Renaissance maker needs to get very comfortable with.

You know, it's all right. When you were just an engineer or a developer or someone who started off at an elementary level, you are just going through the rungs and coming up to mid-level management. But the moment you become a manager, you become assigned to some degree of leadership. You need to start changing gears and think what strategy skills should I be thinking of using in my day to day work? Unfortunately, because you come from a subject matter expertise or you are an engineer or you started off at the ground level, the center of gravity almost pulls you back to where you started. In a sense, you are so comfortable doing things, but to make the mental switch to becoming a strategic leader calls for some degree of an effort.

So all were the strategies that if you have to be seen as a leader, why? Because as you go up the ranks, you are no longer just be or rewarded for what you do, but how you harness everybody around you, how you harness the resources given to you and how you keep your eyes and focus on the game, which is customer delight and delivery of success in a project or whatever. Are the strategic goals that you as a leader sign up for? One of the difficult parts about strategy making is the constant impulse to go into tactics, tactics that are important without action, nothing matters. The best strategy goes waste if you don't get down to the brass tacks and get it going. I understand that. But a leader's time is better spent constantly as a thinker, thinking of strategic moves.

This, this. It's a tough area to be in because it involves scenario planning. It involves thinking about what my options are. It involves thinking. And thinking is a very hard task these days with the amount of pressure on our time, with the amount of pressure on our meetings, with the amount of pressure. Well, your calendar is back to back meetings. Where do you get time to think strategically? And that's where having some degree of time, blocks or time chunks just to refresh and reflect on your strategy is very important. I usually use my weekends and Saturdays and Sundays to actually plan for the strategy of the week ahead, because in the week I will never get a moment to reflect back on my strategy or even when I'm doing something unrelated to work.

I am kind of reflecting on that because thinking involves dedicated mental stamina. If you do not have the mental bandwidth and the stamina to grapple with the problem, then you're not cut out for strategy for doing you're a good implementer, you are a good doer. But from doing to leading is a significant leap. And that's where leaders, Renaissance leaders, need to have the strategy always on their head thinking, how will this affect me? How will this affect my unit? How will this affect my team? How will it affect my larger organization? How will it affect my customers? How will it affect our senior leaders? How will it affect our marketing, our media presence and so on? And so what's the ability to think from a variety of angles is strategy.

Strategy is just thinking of the big picture and playing out scenarios. You know, going back to this every game in one strategy, the NFL thrives on playbooks and so on. So everybody's big on strategy, but the ability to think multiple moves ahead, the ability to anticipate competitor moves, the ability to do what if analysis comes from a strong strategy background. So I want to challenge all the leaders in this book, whoever you are taking this book, if you want to be a good Renaissance leader, you need to build your strategic skills always with the strategies, skills and think like a CEO, think like a CFO, things like a CMO, think like a top leader and say, therefore, what does this mean for my organization?

A Leader Has A Heart - And Often Is Not Afraid To Wear It On His Sleeve

Another role that pioneering leaders play, and this is something that most people are not comfortable with, is one of a nurse, a motherly role or a sort of a psychologist shrink back. What do I mean by that half of the time you are in leadership is dealing with the messy interpersonal insecurities and other emotional related problems inside of teams. You know, every time you bring three or four people into a team, there are a whole lot of strengths. But there are also a whole lot of dysfunctional aspects that come out in a team setting. And as a team, as a leader, you get drawn into these settings about how he did this. She did this. She said she insulted me.

I heard some of that almost like, you know, elementary school, middle school type of bickering that goes on in teams. And you kind of take a deep breath often and just say. Let's redraw the boundaries. Let's reset some lines, bring them into a conversation, and half the time one person comes to you and says something and another person comes and sees something completely different about the same person. So you just play the referee all the time and so much of your time is lost in that as well. But it's an inevitable aspect of team management and people management.

So how do you manage those interpersonal conflicts is a big part of your leadership journey? You can't be unless you can't be this shrink who listens to people waiting out at you, who listens to you. You're also playing the role of a coach and a referee who's trying to bring them so. Whether you like it or not, managing people is a messy aspect. Some people are so comfortable just doing their things on the computer, but it doesn't really matter. What matters is when you are a leader, you have to deal with people. And as you deal with people, you discover that this is nothing related. You know, how to cajole them, how to coach them and how to comfortably manage their emotions comes into play.

How comfortable are you when people come in and just keep bickering and they come to you because you are the boss, you are the leader, you are the supervisor, and if you do wish you can do it, then you're abdicating your role as a leader. I once had a boss. Any time somebody came to him with a complaint, he would immediately call the other person and make them talk in front of them. And sometimes that works. That's the best way to deal with it. But there are also times when you just need to hear them out, give them a lending ear and. And soon enough, when you play that empathetic nurse role, people often feel that they are understood and they go back and resolve it. So they are depending on the complexity and the intensity of the emotion. You need to play this role as a nurse. Do you have enough capacity to listen to others' feelings and manage conflict at the workplace?

The Fixer- Leader Is Always Asking The Question - How Can We Fix It And Up

Another skill that is very important for Iran as its leader is being this handy man in being this fixer in this me in being this reporter and being this the SWAT team, no matter which metaphor, you use a handyman metaphor on the SWAT team that that we see all too often, both in the entertainment world and in the military world, is just the ability to parachute your way into a troublesome situation and then just do diagnosis, prescription resolution and exit very quick and dirty type of play where you come in, roll up your sleeves and just do some transformative work and leave the scene. Many times I was called into crisis settings because of that kind of a skill that I brought to the office. I enjoyed it, I mean, I don't enjoy crises. I mean, it puts me in high pressure situations.

But some of my best performance came when I got pulled into a crisis and that involved me pulling out all stops and pulling in favors from people, calling people that we knew, building relationships with people which you did not know in that crisis, or a whole set of skills involved in crisis management. As a result of some of those troubleshooting and diagnostics that I've done, I built a sort of a reputation to beat this crisis manager or reputation repair of sorts wherever I went. Even today, many years later, people still talk about how I was involved in some high profile cases. Back then, that company that started was going through a growth phase.

You need to also have this ability to paratroop into situations like that, you are called to be this fixer, are troubleshooter or SWAT team member, whatever metaphor, right. So how good you are in those crisis settings sets you up for future leadership? I got many good opportunities because of the way I held my comm. I worked with people around me when they were losing their ads and came in, came out in flying colors. As a result of these crises, every organization is going through a similar crisis because of the pandemic.

If you're a Renaissance leader, you will constantly be looking out for those crises and see how we can use this crisis to develop a strong position for the company? How can we leverage these difficult moments and turn it around for benefits for the company? There's a saying that says, never waste a crisis, never don't let a crisis go to waste in that no matter what happens, there is an upside to it. There is a silver lining to it that if you capture it, can stand you in good stead. So take a moment and ask yourself, how good are you in crisis situations? How can you embrace this crisis mindset in a positive, proactive way and look for opportunities as you brace for impact and deal with that kind of difficulty? Take a moment to reflect on your own crisis capability and see if you fit into that crisis manager role of a leader.

A Leader Is Always Brokering, Partnering And Making Alliances

The second skill or another skill that is very important to being a good Renaissance leader is making deals, making partnerships, making alliances, making exchanges. You know, in many ways your job as a leader, emerging leaders, big leader is about making deals. It's about being a diplomat, you know, every country has diplomats sent to other countries. Right. The job of that diplomat is to represent that country's interests in the country that this diplomat goes into. So in many ways, your role as a leader is to be that diplomat for your unit, for your team, for your organization. So let's say you go to an industry event, even though it is not right in your area, you should be thinking about how you might represent your company in that event, even though it's not part of your job.

You should be thinking, hey, should I be meeting people and just collect those business cards and give it to my marketing team? Should I be doing this and see if I can build some alliances with somebody? Should I think of going and attending this event? And in other words, you think like a brand ambassador that what ambassador is used again in a diplomatic setting very often is that a certain ambassador of a country is representing that country's interests in a country that he goes to. So every leader is a brand ambassador, every leader is a deal maker. Every leader is a dealer who's constantly scouting for opportunities, even if they don't happen to be directly in your job description.

You know, the times that I won brownie points with my other colleagues was at times like these that I bump into someone I bump into, I meet people somewhere and we talk and we exchange business cards and I come back and connect those guys and say, this might be of interest to you and those connections. They stay on unlinked and they stay on on your Rolodex, if you are still in the old school of Rolodex and connecting cards and so on. What matters is, are you showing that this position, that inclination of a brand ambassador of a leader was constantly looking to make these? Take a moment to reflect on this skill that is so important to every leader.

This New Age Leader Is A Pathfinder And Pathmaker

Another rule that every other Nationals leader has to put on is one called a port breaker, a pioneer, a trailblazer, someone who sort of goes first and clears the Bushes, who is somebody who sets up the teams that are coming behind him for success. What do I mean by that? A couple of times in my career journey, I was enlisted into teams such as that to either in a merger or acquisition situation or even in a time there was a crisis situation. You are expected to go and use your skills to sort of clear the bushes for everybody else. Those kinds of leaders who can adapt to this kind of a pioneer setting just literally walk into the unknown. They are totally comfortable with the unknown, totally comfortable with the uncertainty, totally comfortable with the ambiguity that goes along with this unknown terrain. And as a result, they are backing themselves in a very deep manner.

I mean, just imagine the stakes and more, as well as the responsibility and the pressure of just walking into this unknown situation where you have no idea what it is going to be. It calls for a deep rooted confidence on the part of the leader to be able to say, you know what, I've been. Doing this kind of stuff in my past, so my past will become a source of strength for me as I handle the unknown future. So that pioneering spirit comes from a lot of past successes and lost confidence. And because of that past successes and confidence, they are enlisted in the first place, and so it's sort of a cycle that self-confidence begets more confidence and that assurance sets them up for the future. And as you can pretty much imagine, these guys thrive on these kinds of challenges.

I have a colleague who I admire immensely who has this track record of going into these kinds of Problem-Solving situations and has tried consistently over the years in those kinds of settings. We enjoy conversing about those experiences because I kind of sense the adventure that he goes through every time. And we all kind of enjoy doing some of those kinds of projects together. Your comfort level with the unknown actually sets you up for success in this kind of a pathbreaking, trailblazing, pioneering type of a role. When was the last time you took on a pioneering role in anything relating to your field if there's a new technology that is coming? Are you willing to say, you know.

I want to bet some of my time and resources on that and go into that area and become a pioneer? That is what is called a pioneer and developing people. Can you take some people in your team and say, hey, there's this technology of this trend that I'm seeing in the marketplace. This is what our customers are seeing. We should be ready and pull some people and set up a pioneering team and build them to take their bets into the future. That is a pioneer. Take a moment to reflect on your own capacity to do pioneering work.

The Difference Between A Leader And Coach Is Exponential

And the final rule every Renaissance leader has to play is served to be a coach. What do I mean by being a coach? A leader's role often just is a combination of a mentor, coach, shrink, nurse, a provider, a traffic cop, often just directing traffic like a very complex, every complex phenomena. There are many complex dimensions to it, but one of the most notable ones is the one of a coach. You know, the most effective coaches are the coaches who have played the game themselves. Not every player can be a great coach, but every great coach has to be a player. In that they are able to relate to each other. The team members, and then draw from their own personal experiences and insights and put that experience and wisdom together to draw even better stuff from the the team, the organization, the unit, whichever level of leadership that that leader is leading.

I had the joy of coaching many young people for a long period of time and often. What your coach does not necessarily translate into strategy and performance on on any given match or on any given day. And that's where a coach's ability to start off feeling the way around each player comes in. You know, one of my greatest joys is to see how some of the coaching that I give to people when they're deployed in the right place, how it pays off and how they come back and say, hey, this worked. Thank you so much for this. A coach's greatest joy is to see his play or his own signature plays come to fruition through the players that he sends out onto the field.

How good are you at coaching, how good are you taking your own practical insights and conveying to others simple, tillable concepts and ideas? Because there's a thinking dimension, too, to this? Because, like I said, you may be a great leader, you may be a good doer, but you can never be a good coaching type of a leader who can serve your team by giving intelligent inputs without putting them on the defensive. And that's where that soft aspect of a coach comes in. Now, we are a sports obsessed nation and we all know how the coaches are such a significant part of team success.

But yet in corporate America or in the business world or in the world of entrepreneurs, we often see failed leadership because people don't often realize that it is just the same team of human beings that are at play here in a different city. So. You've got to think of your role as a coach and start analyzing how you can translate some of your experiences and convert them into distilled, crisp insights that you can allow your team to be coached and more along. Take a moment to see if you have it in you to be a good coach.

www.ingramcontent.com/pod-product-compliance
Lightning Source LLC
Chambersburg PA
CBHW071925210526
45479CB00002B/561